D1356742

Cause Célèbre

By the same author

FRENCH WITHOUT TEARS
FLARE PATH
WHILE THE SUN SHINES
LOVE IN IDLENESS (O MISTRESS MINE)
THE WINSLOW BOY
THE BROWNING VERSION
HARLEQUINADE
ADVENTURE STORY
WHO IS SYLVIA?
THE DEEP BLUE SEA
SEPARATE TABLES
VARIATION ON A THEME
ROSS
THE SLEEPING PRINCE
HEART TO HEART *(A play for television)*
MAN AND BOY
A BEQUEST TO THE NATION
IN PRAISE OF LOVE
(with a curtain-raiser BEFORE DAWN*)*

Cause Célèbre

A PLAY IN TWO ACTS BY

TERENCE RATTIGAN

HAMISH HAMILTON

LONDON

30838

820-2 RAT

First published in Great Britain 1978
by Hamish Hamilton Limited
90 Great Russell Street London WC1B 3PT
Second impression June 1978

Copyright © 1977, 1978 by Terence Rattigan

All professional performing rights in *Cause Célèbre*
are controlled by Dr Jan van Loewen Ltd.,
81/83 Shaftesbury Avenue, London W1

Amateur performing rights are controlled by
Samuel French Ltd., 26 Southampton Street, Strand,
London WC2

British Library Cataloguing in Publication Data

Rattigan, Sir Terence
  Cause Célèbre.
  I. Title
  822'.9'12   PR6035.A75
  ISBN 0-241-89868-4

Printed and bound in Great Britain by
REDWOOD BURN LIMITED
Trowbridge & Esher

Cause Célèbre opened at Her Majesty's Theatre in London on Monday 4th July 1977, presented by John Gale.

The director of the production was Robin Midgley, the designer Adrian Vaux and the cast was:

ALMA RATTENBURY	Glynis Johns
FRANCIS RATTENBURY	Anthony Pedley
CHRISTOPHER	Matthew Ryan *or*
	Douglas Melbourne
IRENE RIGGS	Sheila Grant
GEORGE WOOD	Neil Daglish
EDITH DAVENPORT	Helen Lindsay
JOHN DAVENPORT	Jeremy Hawk
TONY DAVENPORT	Adam Richardson
STELLA MORRISON	Angela Browne
RANDOLPH BROWN	Kevin Hart
JUDGE	Patrick Barr
O'CONNOR	Kenneth Griffith
CROOM-JOHNSON	Bernard Archard
CASSWELL	Darryl Forbes-Dawson
MONTAGU	Philip Bowen
CLERK OF THE COURT	David Glover
JOAN WEBSTER	Peggy Aitchison
SERGEANT BAGWELL	Anthony Pedley
PORTER	Anthony Howard
WARDER	David Masterman
CORONER	David Glover

The action of the play takes place in Bournemouth and London in 1934 and 1935.

This play was inspired by the facts of a well-known case, but the characters attributed to the individuals represented are based on the author's imagination, and are not necessarily factual.

To
PEGS
with love and gratitude

ACT ONE

The stage represents at various times Court Number One at the Old Bailey and other parts of the Central Criminal Court in London, a villa at Bournemouth, the drawing-room of a flat in Kensington and other places. Changes of scene are effected mainly by lighting, the curtain falling only at the end of each of the two acts.

Lights on ALMA *and* MRS. DAVENPORT. *After a moment, light comes up very dimly on the* CLERK OF THE COURT.

CLERK OF THE COURT. Alma Victoria Rattenbury you are charged with the murder of Francis Mawson Rattenbury on March the twenty eighth 1935. Are you guilty or not guilty?

ALMA. *(almost inaudibly)* Not guilty.

The lights *change as the* CLERK OF THE COURT *turns towards* MRS. DAVENPORT.

CLERK OF THE COURT. Edith Amelia Davenport, take the book in your right hand and read what is on this card.

The light on the CLERK OF THE COURT *slowly fades out.*

MRS. DAVENPORT. I do solemnly swear by Almighty God that I will well and truly try the issues joined between our sovereign Lord the King and the prisoners at the bar and will give a true verdict according to the evidence.

The spots fade *out on* ALMA *and* MRS. DAVENPORT.

MRS. DAVENPORT *and* STELLA MORRISON *in the sitting-room of the flat in Kensington.* STELLA *is* MRS. DAVENPORT'S *sister, a year or two younger.*

STELLA. A jury summons!—my dear, how too frightful. Let's see.

MRS. DAVENPORT *hands her the official letter.*

(reading) '. . . present yourself at the . . . jury service . . . for fifteen days . . . and fail not at your peril'—indeed!

MRS. DAVENPORT. *(smiling)* Yes, rather scaring that. Peril of what d'you think? Hard labour, or the stocks, or just a ducking?

STELLA. Whopping great fine, I should think. Might almost be worth paying it—I'll get Henry to cough up the necessary if you like.

MRS. DAVENPORT. *(taking back the letter)* Certainly not. I'm quite looking forward to it, as it happens.

STELLA. What, a whole fortnight?

MRS. DAVENPORT. Well, I've got the time these days, and who knows, I might do a bit of good for some old soul who's snitched a pair of silk stockings from Barkers.

STELLA. More likely to be indecent exposure.

MRS. DAVENPORT. Oh, they wouldn't have women on those juries, would they?

STELLA. My dear, they have women on everything these days.

MRS. DAVENPORT. Well if it is that, I'll just have to face it like

3

—well, like a man, I suppose. But I'm not going on that date—I'm not going to mess up Tony's Christmas hols. I'll ask for a postponement to May, that should be safe.

STELLA. Is he enjoying himself in Cannes?

MRS. DAVENPORT. Tony? He says so in his postcards, but I expect they're written under John's supervision. Thank Heavens it's the last time.

STELLA. You're still determined on the divorce?

MRS. DAVENPORT. Yes. Quite.

STELLA. Well, you know what I think.

MRS. DAVENPORT. A separation doesn't give me custody.

STELLA. You won't get *complete* custody.

MRS. DAVENPORT. Oh yes I will. John won't defend it. He's too scared of his Under Secretary. It'll all be fixed out of court. If he does defend it, I'll win.

STELLA. There was only that one woman, wasn't there?

MRS. DAVENPORT. Oh, no. In the five years before we separated I've found out now there were at least two others. And now there's this dreadful woman.

STELLA. Still, four in five years? That doesn't really make him Bluebeard, you know. In fact for most husbands with un-willing wives I'd say it was about par for the course.

MRS. DAVENPORT. Are you trying to make it my fault again?

STELLA. Well he was only about forty, wasn't he, when you started having headaches? That *is* a bit young, darling, for a husband to find himself in the spare room.

MRS. DAVENPORT. I couldn't go on, Stella. I told you. I never did care much for that side of things, as you know, and as he got older he got more and more demanding.

STELLA. That's one thing I could never say about Henry—

MRS. DAVENPORT. He used to say that my reluctance made him want it more. Now you can't say that's normal, Stella.

STELLA. I suppose not—I just wonder if it would work with Henry. . . . How does Tony feel about it all? He always seemed to be quite fond of his father.

MRS. DAVENPORT. Well, he was. Of course now that I've told him the truth—not all of it, of course, just enough—he's beginning to see things my way. Unless he's been led astray these last two weeks. I wouldn't put anything past that man. I really hate him.

FADE OUT

4

DAVENPORT. There should be a car waiting to pick me up. The name's Davenport—would you put that one down there and come back for the other?

PORTER. Very good, sir! (*He exits*)

DAVENPORT. Well, Tony, I'm afraid this is goodbye. You had better take the Airport bus to Victoria Air Terminus, and get a taxi to Kensington from there . . . I'm going straight to the Home Office, so—

TONY. (*quickly*) I understand. (*Pause*) Dad, I will be seeing you again, won't I?

DAVENPORT. Well, certainly in court.

TONY. I meant after that?

DAVENPORT. I'm afraid that depends on your mother.

TONY. I see. Can I ask one thing?

DAVENPORT. Yes.

TONY. Mum always talks to me—well sometimes talks to me—about *that* woman, etcetera etcetera!

DAVENPORT. Yes.

TONY. Well—there isn't any *that* woman, is there? I mean, I've been with you two weeks, and I'm not half-witted . . .

DAVENPORT. No, you're not.

TONY. You still love Mum, don't you?

DAVENPORT. Yes, I do.

TONY. Dad—is there any *that* woman?

Pause.

PORTER. I've found your car, sir; do you want the other one in the boot?

DAVENPORT. No, my son is travelling by the bus, so—

PORTER. Yes, sir. I'll get him a place.

TONY. Thank you.

DAVENPORT. I'll do the V.I.P. Well, goodbye, Tony.

TONY. Thank you for a marvellous time.

DAVENPORT. A bit dull, I'm afraid.

TONY. Not Cannes. That was smashing.

DAVENPORT. You didn't like Paris?

TONY. Well, don't think I'm ungrateful, Dad, but you did promise to take me to a—to a—you know—that 'House of all Nations'—

DAVENPORT. Tony I did remember that. It's just that—well, you have to take a passport, you see.

TONY. A passport to a brothel?

5

DAVENPORT. They're very strict about under age.

TONY. (*despairing*) Oh Dad! Even in France? I'll have to try Turkey or somewhere.

DAVENPORT. (*laughing*) Why Turkey? Why not here—Jermyn Street?

TONY. I'd thought of that, only I'm a bit—well—

DAVENPORT. I'm not serious. At least, not yet. I should give it another year or two, I think old chap, don't you?

TONY. But Dad I'm seventeen!

DAVENPORT. Yes, but that's still a bit young, don't you think? My first wasn't till I was twenty. But still, when you do go, for God's sake take precautions, won't you?

TONY. What—?

PORTER. I've got your place, sir.

DAVENPORT. Thank you. (*Gives him half a crown*)

PORTER. Thank you, sir. (*He goes*)

DAVENPORT. Well—

TONY. Dad, what shall I tell Mum—about *that* woman?

DAVENPORT. Tell her you didn't meet her, but I was always talking to her on the telephone. It's a question of her pride. Off you go, Tony.

WOOD *crosses the stage to stand outside the* RATTENBURYS' *house, taking off his bicycle clips.*

The lights COME UP *to show the hall, sitting-room, stairs.* IRENE RIGGS, *maid and companion to* ALMA—*dressed more as companion than maid—is entering the tiny hall.*

IRENE. Yes? What is it?

WOOD. I've come about the advert.

IRENE. You're too old.

WOOD. It says fourteen to eighteen.

IRENE. I know what it says. I wrote it myself. You're too old.

WOOD. I'm seventeen.

IRENE. You're still not what we're wanting. Sorry.

ALMA. (*calling from upstairs*) Who is it, Irene?

IRENE. (*calling back*) A boy about the advert. He's wrong.

ALMA. (*calling*) Why?

IRENE. (*calling*) He's too old.

WOOD. (*making his voice heard aloft*) I'm not. I'm only seventeen.

IRENE. (*calling*) But he looks much older.

6

ALMA. (*after a pause—calling*) I'll come down.

IRENE. (*calling*) I was sending him away.

ALMA. (*decisively*) Keep him.

IRENE (*annoyed, to* WOOD) You'd better come in. (*clicking her tongue*) You're not the type at all.

ALMA *has meanwhile swung her legs off the bed.*

ALMA (*calling*) I'll just slip into something. I won't be a mo.

Pulls out a pair of day pyjamas—of a fairly hectic design and colour—from the wardrobe.

Downstairs WOOD *has come in and is waiting uncertainly in the hall, twisting his homburg hat.*

(*calling*) Tell him to go into the lounge, Irene, and make himself comfortable.

IRENE (*nodding towards the sitting-room*) You heard her.

WOOD (*on his way in*) You the maid?

IRENE. Companion.

WOOD. You don't like me, do you?

IRENE. I've nothing against you. You're just not the type, that's all.

WOOD. That'll be for her to say, won't it?

He nods upstairs. IRENE *regards him coldly.*

IRENE. (*at length*) Yes, it will.

She goes down the passage and disappears. WOOD *looks round the sitting-room and perches on a chair. Upstairs* ALMA *has finished her dressing and is applying lipstick, then patting her hair into place.* WOOD *gets up and goes to a small piano, on the stand of which is a piece of sheet music left open. He examines it.* ALMA *comes rapidly down the stairs in slippered feet and surprises him as she comes in. He starts guiltily away from the piano.*

WOOD. Sorry.

ALMA. (*laughing*) That's quite all right. I don't mind anyone reading my music.

WOOD. Oh, I don't read music. Did you say *your* music?

ALMA. Look at the front.

WOOD. (*awed*) That's a picture of you.

ALMA. Taken a long time ago, I'm afraid. It's twelve years old, that photograph.

WOOD. 'Dark-Haired Marie' by Lozanne. Is that you—Miss Lozanne?

ALMA. Oh no—that's just my pen-name.

Seeing WOOD's *bewilderment.*

7

It's just the name I put on my songs. My real name's Alma. What's yours?

WOOD. Wood.

ALMA. Christian name?

WOOD. Perce. Percy really. My Dad calls me Perce—so Perce.

ALMA. What does your Dad do for a living?

WOOD. He's a builder, laid off. I work for him when he's got work—but there's not much of that about these days.

ALMA. Oh I know. It's terrible this slump. I can't sell a song these days—for love nor money.

WOOD. Do you do this for a living, Miss?

ALMA. Oh no. I don't have to, thank heavens, or I'd be on the dole. Mind you they do get done sometimes. That song, for instance, that was done only a year ago, on the B.B.C. A baritone sang it.

WOOD. (*eagerly*) The Whispering Baritone?

ALMA. No. Just a baritone. Let me take your cap.

WOOD. Thank you, Miss.

She takes it from him and puts it on the piano.

ALMA. By the way, it's Mrs. Mrs. three times over, as it happens—

WOOD. Cor. Divorced?

ALMA. (*gaily*) Yes once, the other one died and now seven years gone with old Ratz—Mr. Rattenbury, my present one. I'm giving things away, aren't I? I started very young. I've a boy of thirteen. Almost as old as you.

She laughs. He smiles politely.

Yes, well . . . I suppose it's working on building sites that's made you so—developed.

WOOD. I bike a lot too.

ALMA. Yes. That does do wonders for the physique. You look quite what I would call—full-grown.

Pause. WOOD *has at last dimly realised the nature of his future mistress's interest in him.*

WOOD. Your—Irene—thought I was too full-grown.

ALMA. Yes. Well you see we concocted that advertisement together, and what *she* had in mind was—well—a rather smaller kind of boy. You'd be under her, really, not me . . . Well I'd better tell you what the wages are. It's one of the reasons we wanted a little boy. I'm afraid my husband will only go to a pound a week.

8

WOOD. Living in?

ALMA. No, I'm afraid not. We haven't room really. There's only one other room besides Irene's you see, and my two boys—I've another little one, only six—well they're in there, during school holidays that is. Of course if you'd been a little boy like I meant in the advert, you *could* have slept in with them—I mean, if you'd been a really *little* boy—but being as you are, and me and Irene slipping about upstairs with next to nothing on—well it would be rather awkward, wouldn't it? . . . (*Rather breathlessly*) No, I'm afraid living in's quite out of the question.

WOOD. I was only asking. Where does old Ratz sleep?

ALMA. Oh, you mustn't call him Ratz. You must call him Mr. Rattenbury, like Irene.

WOOD. Yes. Where does he sleep?

Pause.

ALMA. Inquisitive, aren't you? That's all right. I like an enquiring nature. Mr. Rattenbury sleeps through there.

She points to the door off the sitting-room.

He can't do the stairs any more.

Pause.

WOOD. I see.

ALMA. (*lightly, after another pause*) Well, is it a go, or isn't it?

WOOD. A quid isn't much.

ALMA. Well, I could slip you a few bob on the side—expenses, you know. Only Ratz—Mr. Rattenbury mustn't know. He's a little strict about money. Do you live close?

WOOD. Other side of Bournemouth. About half hour on my bike. You wouldn't like to say how many bob?

ALMA. (*patting his arm*) You must ask when you need it.

WOOD. O.K.

ALMA. Well I'm glad that's settled. Why don't we have a little drinkie on it?

WOOD. I'm afraid I don't drink.

ALMA. I expect that's just what you tell all your employers. Gin and it?

WOOD. I don't know what that is.

ALMA. Fancy anyone not knowing what a ' gin and it' is!

She is busy pouring herself a drink.

. . . Won't you just try a sip, just to seal our little arrangement?

WOOD. If you insist.

ALMA. Oh I don't *insist*. I never insist. But just this once—

9

There has to be a first time for everything, doesn't there?

WOOD. Yes.

ALMA. A little of what you fancy's my motto, and a very good one too. This is a lovely world we're in, and we were put into it to enjoy it. Don't you agree?

She hands him the drink.

WOOD. I might. I don't think my Dad would. He's religious.

ALMA. Well our dear Lord didn't say we mustn't have fun, did He? He turned water into wine, not wine into water. Just tell that to your Dad next time he gets narky. And He said we must love each other, and I think we should.

Raising her glass.

Well, Perce—no I can't call you Perce. Or Percy. Have you got a middle name?

WOOD. George.

ALMA. That's nice. I'm going to call you that. (*Raising her glass again*) George.

WOOD. (*raising his*) Mrs. Rattenbury.

ALMA. Alma . . . Not just now—always . . .

WOOD. Alma.

ALMA. George!

They drink. WOOD *makes a face.* ALMA *laughs and takes the glass away from him.*

I'm not letting you have any more. I'm not having anyone say I'm leading you astray.

She drinks WOOD's *drink in a single gulp.*

Just like water to me. Do you know what Alma means in Latin? A professor told me once, it means life-giving, bountiful. In olden times they used it about goddesses, like Venus.

Sipping her drink.

Well I'm not Venus, God knows—but apparently it also means kind and comforting, and that I am, George, though I say it who shouldn't—

RATTENBURY *comes into the hall.*

Here's Ratz. I'd better warn you. You have to shout.

She opens the sitting-room door. RATTENBURY *immediately glances at* WOOD. *Deaf he may be, but certainly not blind.* ALMA *kisses him.*

(*loudly*) Had a nice walkie?

RATTENBURY. There was an east wind. You should have told me.

ALMA. Poor thing, did you get chilled?

RATTENBURY. Blasted to buggery.

Paying no attention to WOOD, *he sits down in what is evidently his usual armchair—significantly one that has its back to a pair of French windows.*

RATTENBURY. Get me a whiskey, would you?

ALMA. It's a bit early for your whiskey, isn't it?

She begins to get him a drink.

RATTENBURY. It's a bit early for your gin.

ALMA. I only meant you don't usually have whiskey in the mornings.

RATTENBURY. I don't usually get blasted to buggery in the morning.

Showing a paper.

Shares are down again.

ALMA. Oh dear. You're probably wondering who the stranger is.

RATTENBURY. No, I wasn't, but who is he?

ALMA. His name is George Wood, and he's the new help.

RATTENBURY. (*after a moody sip*) Irene said a boy.

ALMA. Well he *is* a boy. He's only seventeen.

RATTENBURY. Hm.

He stares at WOOD *without overmuch interest.*

Has he any references?

WOOD. No, sir. I've never done this kind of work before.

RATTENBURY. What?

ALMA. (*putting her hand on his shoulder*) Don't worry dear. We had a nice long interview. I'll vouch for him.

RATTENBURY *looks up at her. He grunts acquiescence and hands her his glass.*

That one went down pretty fast.

RATTENBURY. Not as fast as my shares.

As she passes WOOD

Does he drive?

WOOD. (*loudly*) Yes, sir. I've got a licence.

ALMA. (*coming back with the whiskey*) Well isn't that marvellous! (*To* RATTENBURY, *loudly*) Isn't that handy, dear? We've got ourselves a chauffeur.

RATTENBURY. No uniform.

ALMA. (*loudly*) No, of course not. (*To* WOOD, *quietly*) Well, perhaps a cap and a smart mackintosh. You'd look nice in a cap.

RATTENBURY. What are you saying?

ALMA. I was explaining no uniform, dear. (*To* WOOD) Better go now. (*Loudly*) I'm just showing the new help to the front door.

ALMA. (*to* WOOD) Come on. (*To* RATTENBURY) Back in a jiffy.

She and WOOD *go.*

—Well that's settled, thank goodness. It's lovely about your driving. Go and buy yourself a cap. (*She fishes in her bag*) Here's fifteen shillings. Will that be enough?

WOOD. Should be.

CHRISTOPHER *comes in, wearing his scout's uniform.*

CHRISTOPHER. Mummy, there's a smashing bike outside, with low handlebars. (*Seeing* WOOD) Oh, is it yours, sir?

WOOD. Yes. A Raleigh.

CHRISTOPHER. I was going to ask if I could ride it.

WOOD. Afraid I'm just going.

ALMA. But he's coming back tomorrow—and every day afterwards. He's going to be one of the family.

CHRISTOPHER. Oh good.

ALMA. I'm sure if you ask him nicely he'll let you ride it.

WOOD. You bet.

CHRISTOPHER. Oh thanks awfully, sir. Mummy, when's lunch?

ALMA. Quite soon, darling.

CHRISTOPHER (*calling and running off*) Irene!

CHRISTOPHER *disappears up the stairs.*

ALMA. Sweet, isn't he? (*Sincerely*) I really am very blessed with my children.

WOOD. (*in awe*) He called me sir.

ALMA. What? (*Misunderstanding*) Oh they teach him that at his school. Don't worry. He'll soon be calling you George.

WOOD. I'd rather he went on calling me sir.

ALMA. I'll see he does then.

IRENE *appears from the shadows.*

(*hastily to* WOOD) Goodbye then. I'll see you tomorrow.

WOOD. What time?

ALMA. What time, Irene?

Pause.

IRENE. (*at length, gloomily*) Seven. Not a second later.

ALMA. Can you manage seven?

WOOD. Easy . . . Be seeing you.

He goes out. ALMA, *left alone with* IRENE, *is uneasy under her steady stare.*

IRENE. (*at length*) You'll have my notice at the end of the week.

ALMA *laughs and embraces her fondly.*

ALMA. Yes, darling, I'm sure I will.

IRENE. I'm serious.

ALMA. You always are. He can drive, Irene, which is more than any of your little teenies could have done.

IRENE. Yes. There's something else he can do that my little teenies couldn't.

ALMA. ᵼ Irene . . .

IRENE. Anyway you owe me four weeks' wages.

ALMA. Six pounds?

She looks in her bag.

Oh dear. And there's Christopher's new cricket bat. (*Nodding towards sitting-room*) He's in a bad mood . . . still he's got a couple of whiskies inside him. Think of something for me—

IRENE. I don't know.

ALMA. Pray for me.

IRENE. Yes.

She goes into the sitting-room. IRENE *exits.*

ALMA *goes up to* RATTENBURY.

ALMA. (*to* RATTENBURY, *brightly*) Well Ratz, darling. Let me get you another little drinkie. There's time for one before lunch.

She takes his now empty glass to refill it.

(*loudly*) I've been showing George the car.

RATTENBURY. Who's George?

ALMA. Our new chauffeur, darling . . . (*She brings the drink to him*) He says it's in spanking condition, except just for one little thing—(*She sits down, smiling lovingly*)—it needs a new carburettor. He says if we don't have one the car might seize up altogether, and that would mean a new car, darling.

RATTENBURY. Well we'll have to walk then, won't we?

ALMA. (*laughing merrily*) Oh you are a scream . . .

RATTENBURY. (*he chokes on his drink*) This is too strong.

ALMA *takes the glass and puts more water in it.*

ALMA. Now after lunch we'll get your cheque book out and write out a cheque.

RATTENBURY. I won't sign it.

She comes back with the drink, and lays her hand lovingly on his head.

ALMA. Oh yes you will, dear. You're far too kind and loving a husband not to. (*She kisses the top of his head*) Oh I do love my darling Ratz.

THE LIGHTS FADE

13

TONY. Mum! Listen to this—Did you know Mrs. Rattenbury and Wood battered old Rattenbury on the head so hard they completely smashed his skull.

MRS. DAVENPORT. What? Oh you're reading about that awful murder. A few years ago, a case like that wouldn't even have been mentioned in *The Times* . . . be a darling . . .

TONY. That's what makes it so funny it happening in Bournemouth.

MRS. DAVENPORT. I don't see that that's funny.

TONY. On Aunt Stella's doorstep . . . And ours, when we get that house. I wonder what their defence will be. Wood's statement says he was doped on cocaine, and the police say Mrs. Rattenbury was as drunk as a fly.

MRS. DAVENPORT. Tony, I don't want you to talk about it. And you shouldn't be reading it. Haven't you your homework to do?

TONY. Finished. Mum, could I ask you a question?

MRS. DAVENPORT. Of course.

TONY. If you'd found out before you started the divorce that there wasn't another woman at all with Dad, would it have made any difference?

Pause.

MRS. DAVENPORT. But there is another woman.

TONY. No, there isn't. I'm sure there isn't. And I honestly think he'd come back, if you asked him.

MRS. DAVENPORT. On his terms . . .

TONY. I don't know what they are.

MRS. DAVENPORT. I can't explain it to you, darling. You're far too young to understand . . .

TONY. (*with unexpected vehemence*) That isn't true! Please believe me—I understand much more than you know.

Pause.

MRS. DAVENPORT. . . . Is Randolph coming here, or are you going to him?

TONY. He's coming here.

MRS. DAVENPORT. (*she takes a note from her handbag*) Is ten shillings enough?

TONY. Oh, plenty.

MRS. DAVENPORT. And for the cinema too?

TONY. It's only The Kensington.

MRS. DAVENPORT (*sharply*) What's the film?

TONY. I don't remember the title. It's got Irene Dunne—

MRS. DAVENPORT. (*relieved*) That should be very nice. You haven't told me yet how you like my new dress.

TONY. Spiffing. Who are you out to impress?

MRS. DAVENPORT. Stella's coming to take me to have dinner with General and Lady Whitworth.

TONY. Oh yes. And they're important because of the new house, or something.

MRS. DAVENPORT. He's Chairman of the Bournemouth Country Club, which owns the whole estate—He's a terrible old snob, according to Stella, so I expect it'll be an excruciating evening. A lot of small talk about gout and cricket, and trouble with the under-gardeners.

TONY. Is it worth it?

MRS. DAVENPORT. Oh yes, darling, it's a lovely little house— quite perfect for just the two of us, so I'll have to be a good girl and say all the right things. They're determined only to let in 'a certain class of person'!

TONY. Not Mrs. Rattenbury! (*He laughs*) Oops, sorry.

MRS. DAVENPORT *smiles*.

You don't have to worry, Mum, I'm sure you'll manage your grapefruit perfectly.

MRS. DAVENPORT. And not eat peas with a knife?

TONY. Or tell any of those filthy stories of yours.

He laughs.

MRS. DAVENPORT. (*embracing him*) You're a naughty boy. Your hair needs cutting.

TONY. Tomorrow.

There is a ring at the front door.

MRS. DAVENPORT. Just stay and say hullo, and then leave us alone for a moment, will you? (*Off*) Hello Stella, did you come by car?

She goes out. We hear the sound of greeting in the hall. TONY *fishes out the discarded copy of the* Evening News, *folds it up and puts it into his breast pocket.*

STELLA MORRISON *comes in, also wearing evening dress but, because she is rich, probably a real Chanel rather than a fake Molyneux.*

STELLA. (*as she comes in*) No, I sent the Rolls on ahead and had Phillips pick me up off the train. It wasn't the Belle of course, but it had a perfectly good Pullman—hullo Tony.

TONY. Hullo, Aunt Stella.

He allows himself to be kissed.

STELLA. You get handsomer every time I see you. (*To* MRS. DAVENPORT) Any girls in his life yet?

MRS. DAVENPORT. Oh yes... Happily they all live in Hollywood.

STELLA. (*to* TONY) Wouldn't nearer be better?

MRS. DAVENPORT. (*sharply*) He's too young for girls.

STELLA. Darling, I wasn't being serious. My dear, what about this murder case!

TONY. Did you ever meet her, Aunt Stella?

STELLA. Mrs. Rattenbury? Oh no. But the awful thing is I suppose one could have. Your uncle Henry, of course, is going around boasting he *did* meet her—at a cocktail party somewhere—and she sang one of her songs. But you know what a liar he is. By next week he'll have had an affair with her—

TONY. Which wasn't too difficult, I gather.

STELLA. Difficult for Henry—even with Mrs. Rattenbury. I said to him—you'd better be careful, dear. You don't know what the gardener's boy and I get up to when you're up at the Stock Exchange. We might swing a mallet on you any time—

TONY. (*excitedly*) Do you think they both swung together, or took it in turns? I mean did Wood hit the old boy first and then she finished him off—or—

STELLA. Oh, they both swung together, of course—like two Etonians.

(*singing*)

'And we'll both swing together, and swear by the best of'— what? Not 'schools'—'pools' would do. I gather from the Commissioner there was a pool of blood all over the floor, inches deep—and she was dancing the black bottom in it.

TONY. No, really?

STELLA. Stark naked, my dear, and trying to kiss all the policemen—and shouting out, 'I did it, I did it—I bumped him off!'

MRS. DAVENPORT. (*violently*) Will you please stop!

STELLA *looks at her uneasily. She knows her sister's temperament.*

TONY. Mum's very shocked by it all.

STELLA. Well, of course she is. Of course we all are. (*To her sister*) But with a thing as appalling as this—and in the heart

16

of Bournemouth too—the only thing one can do is to make a joke of it. If one starts trying to think of it seriously, one would go mad. I mean, it being with a servant! To me, that's the real horror.

MRS. DAVENPORT. Tony, go to your room.

TONY. Yes, Mum. (*He kisses* STELLA) Goodbye, Aunt Stella.

MRS. DAVENPORT. Goodnight, darling. (*He kisses her*) I'll try not to disgrace you with the General.

TONY. You'll be a smashing success, I know. (*He goes out*)

MRS. DAVENPORT. To me the real horror is the boy's age—exactly the same age as Tony—

STELLA. When he met her perhaps. Now he's a year older. Eighteen. Old enough to hang.

MRS. DAVENPORT. Oh God! The law's unjust. It's the woman who should hang.

STELLA. Oh, she will. No doubt of that, thank heavens. But after all, the boy did kill his employer. He really shouldn't get away with that.

MRS. DAVENPORT. (*violently*) I don't know. I only know *she* ought to be lynched!

STELLA. Well, she might be. You should hear what they're saying about her in Bournemouth—

MRS. DAVENPORT. I suppose I'm being silly but whenever I think about that horrible case I think about Tony.

STELLA. Yes. I'm afraid you are being rather silly, darling. I doubt if Tony's going to commit murder for a middle-aged nympho-dipso-song-writer. There can't be many in Bournemouth.

MRS. DAVENPORT. (*darkly*) There was a married woman at Dieppe last Christmas, well over thirty, who had an eye on him. French too.

STELLA. Was Tony interested?

MRS. DAVENPORT. I didn't give him a chance to be. I changed hotels.

STELLA. Yes. You would. There are worse ways for a boy to start than with a married woman who knows how to take the right precautions—coupled with a bit of French élan.

MRS. DAVENPORT. Stella!

There is a ring at the front door.

—Just a moment—

She goes out. We hear her voice.

(off) Oh hullo, Randolph.

BROWNE. *(off)* Hullo, Mrs. Davenport.

MRS. DAVENPORT. *(off)* Tony's in his bedroom. You know where that is.

BROWNE. *(off)* Yes. Thank you.

She comes back.

Tony's best pal at Westminster. Randolph Browne. A Bishop's son—and a very good friend for him . . .

STELLA. Well, shall we go?

MRS. DAVENPORT. There's something I want to ask you. Should I mention tonight about John and . . .?

STELLA. Not the bed part—

MRS. DAVENPORT. Really! As if I would—

STELLA. . . . Well don't mention the word divorce tonight. Leave it to me. When's the decree absolute?

MRS. DAVENPORT. Not for another couple of months.

STELLA. Well I hope it's not in the *Bournemouth Echo*—

MRS. DAVENPORT. Stella—after all I am the innocent party.

STELLA. My dear in Bournemouth *nobody* in a divorce is ever the innocent party.

MRS. DAVENPORT. Well let them see me as a glamorous divorcée then.

STELLA. *(as she goes)* Frankly, darling, I don't think that's very likely either.

MRS. DAVENPORT. It's all clear, Tony.

TONY. Thankyou. Goodbye.

FADE *on the sitting-room as they go out, and* FADE UP *on the bedroom, where* RANDOLPH BROWNE, *be-spectacled and studious, sits, deep in the* Evening Standard. *Beside him sits* TONY *deep in his rescued* Evening News. *There is a pause.*

BROWNE. *(at length)* Have you got to the orgy in the Royal Palace Hotel?

TONY. I wonder how many times they did it altogether . . .

BROWNE. From the time he went to live in the house—which was—it's here somewhere—Yes—'Congress first took place a month after he was employed'—

TONY. Congress?

BROWNE. Legal for 'it'.

TONY. What about the Congress of Anglican Bishops? *(As he makes his calculation)* Assuming twice a night for . . .

BROWNE. Why only twice a night? He wasn't in training for anything.

TONY. You mean *you* could have made it more?

BROWNE. Double—Easily.

TONY. Bollocks—Here it is. At twice a night until the murder, three hundred and fourteen times!

BROWNE. You know when they open that trap-door he'll probably float upwards, not drop downwards.

TONY. I'm not being funny, Browne. I really do almost envy him . . .

BROWNE. Mind you, three hundred and fourteen times—That's nothing in a lifetime, and for him it will be a lifetime, poor sod. I hope to put up a million before I die.

TONY. Not a hope. You'll never get enough girls.

BROWNE. You only need one.

TONY. When you're eighty it'll probably still be Jones Minor.

BROWNE. You're out of date.

TONY. Who is it now?

BROWNE. Shuttleworth.

TONY. I don't know him.

BROWNE. He's in the choir.

TONY. God, you are disgusting! Randy by name, and randy by nature.

BROWNE. That's right. Anyway a chap's got to do something, hasn't he? Or else he'd go raving mad.

Pause.

TONY. It's hell, isn't it?

BROWNE. Oh, I don't know. It'll do till something better comes along.

TONY. But when will that be? God, it's frustrating. To be seventeen is hell . . . I mean, seventeen and English and upper-class and living in this century is hell . . . It wasn't always like that. Romeo was only seventeen, Juliet only thirteen.

BROWNE. And a ripe mess they made of things.

TONY. But no one in Shakespeare's time thought they were too *young*, did they? A boy of seventeen and a girl of thirteen? How too utterly disgusting, my dear!

BROWNE. Your mother?

TONY *nods.*

BROWNE. Not a good imitation.

Doing his own imitation evidently of his father.

19

My dear Randolph, should you be troubled with impure thoughts, you will find a cold tub and a brisk trot will work wonders—

TONY. The bishop?

BROWNE. Verbatim.

TONY. I wonder what our parents think we *do* between thirteen and twenty-one.

BROWNE. Solo, I should think, or else have cold tubs and brisk trots.

TONY. It's such damn humbug. Of course they know we're safe—apart from Shuttleworths, which they don't like to think about. You should have heard my mother on this Mrs. Rattenbury. The murder apart, my mother seems to think she's the monster of Glamis, just because she's twenty years older than Wood . . . And why not? Look at her. (*He slaps the paper*) She's damned attractive.

BROWNE. Not bad at all.

TONY. (*muttering*) Three hundred and fourteen times. My God, I've a good mind to—and with Mum out—How much money have you got?

BROWNE. Good mind to what?

TONY. Try it. Tonight.

BROWNE. With Mrs. Rattenbury?

TONY. No, idiot. 'It'.

BROWNE. Oh. (*Counting*) Seventeen and threepence.

TONY. And I've got ten bob. What do you suppose we could get for one pound seven and threepence?

BROWNE. Both of us?

TONY. Don't you want to?

BROWNE. Not for—thirteen and sevenpence halfpenny, thank you.

TONY. Will you lend it to me then?

BROWNE. Are you serious?

TONY. Yes.

BROWNE. I know nothing about it.

He hands him fifteen shillings.

TONY. Why? What can happen to me? She can only say no. (*He goes to the door, and stops nervously*) You won't come with me?

BROWNE. Davenport, you are speaking to the son of a bishop. When I do it it'll be Jermyn Street, and a fiver. I think I should warn you, my dear child, that it's not going to be Romeo and Juliet—or even Wood and Mrs. Rattenbury . . .

The lights *begin to* fade.

TONY. *(calling off)* Be out when Mum gets back.

BROWNE. I'm not staying here!

The lights *now come up to illumine a small cell, at the moment empty. We hear the sound of a metal door being unlocked.*

JOAN. *(off)* In there.

ALMA *comes on. As a remand prisoner she is allowed to wear her own clothes, and she has on a simple but smart dress. She is followed by a wardress (JOAN), a gruff-voiced, rather forbidding woman, younger than ALMA.*

Wait.

She goes across the cell to another unseen door, which we hear opening. Then a murmur of voices. Finally JOAN returns. ALMA meanwhile sits.

I didn't say you could sit.

ALMA. Sorry, dear.

She gets up.

JOAN. If the lawyers allow you to that is their business. I have to obey prison regulations.

ALMA. Yes, of course. What's your name, dear?

JOAN. Wardress Webster.

ALMA. I mean your Christian name.

JOAN. We are not allowed to use first names.

ALMA. Phyllis did. And she used to call me Alma.

JOAN. Who is Phyllis?

ALMA. The other lady. The one that's gone on leave.

JOAN. Oh, Mrs. Stringer. Well, she should not have.

ALMA. Oh I'm sure it was quite wrong. But she was an awful dear, all the same. *(She laughs)* She used to tell me about her little son, same age as my youngest—my little John.

No response from JOAN.

Poor little John . . . Oh well, he doesn't know yet. Christopher —that's my eldest—he does of course. But in his letters he's quite cheerful.

No response from JOAN.

Of course he doesn't quite understand . . .

Her voice trails off.

How long do you think my trial will last?

JOAN. I could not say, I'm sure.

ALMA. Mr. Montagu—such a dear, Mr. Montagu, and so good-looking too—he says it'll last five days. What will I be allowed to wear?

JOAN. It will be your privilege to dress exactly as you please.

ALMA. Could I wear my pyjamas?

JOAN. I would think what you are currently wearing would be more suitable.

ALMA. Oh, I wasn't serious. Phyllis would have seen the joke. No, I mean that's what they always write about. 'The female prisoner, wearing a fetching blue ensemble' . . . Well they did at the Magistrates' Court, anyway. I just can't go on wearing a fetching blue ensemble five days running. I mean on the fifth day it'll stop fetching and start carrying . . .

She laughs gaily. JOAN *does not crack a smile.*

ALMA. (*after a pause*) What made you become a wardress, dear? Did you think you were cut out for it?

JOAN. We are not allowed to answer personal questions.

ALMA. Aren't you? Phyllis always told me—

JOAN. Mrs. Stringer may have had other ideas. I prefer to abide by the rules.

ALMA. Yes—

There is the sound of a metal door opening.

O'CONNOR. (*off*) Thank you, Chief.

JOAN. (*rapping out the order*) Prisoner Rattenbury, on your feet.

ALMA. (*a shade plaintively*) I am on my feet.

O'CONNOR *and* MONTAGU *come in.*

O'CONNOR. (*as they come in*) I don't know . . . quite frankly we'll have our work cut out whoever we get. If we come up at the end of May, it'll probably be Humphreys. Just so long as it isn't Goddard! . . . All right Wardress, you may leave us.

JOAN. Sir.

She marches out.

O'CONNOR. Good morning.

ALMA. Good morning.

O'CONNOR. Sit down, please, Mrs. Rattenbury.

ALMA. Oh thank you—

She sits down. Both barristers sit at a table facing her. O'CONNOR *busily arranges papers in front of him.* MONTAGU, *a young man, opens a packet of cigarettes and offers it to her.*

MONTAGU. Mrs. Rattenbury. (*Offering Players cigarettes*).

ALMA. —Players. My favourites. Oh Mr. Montagu, you are a duck.

He hands her the packet.

MONTAGU. Will those keep you for a time?

ALMA. Oh yes.

MONTAGU. Is there anything else I can get you that you need?

ALMA. Well not really things that a man would know about. Kirbygrips and things. Irene will see to those.

MONTAGU. She's still coming to see you?

ALMA. Oh yes. You can't keep her away.

O'CONNOR. Mrs. Rattenbury, do you persist in saying that your various statements to the police regarding the murder are true?

ALMA. Well, I *can't* go back on them, can I?

O'CONNOR. You can very easily go back on them. In fact, Mrs. Rattenbury, to save your life—I repeat that—to save your life, you must.

ALMA. Mr. O'Connor. I'd like to say the things you want me to say, I really would. But I can't.

O'CONNOR. Very well. Let me read to you some of the official statements you made to the police. Late on the night of the murder, after the body had been removed to hospital, you say to Inspector Mills: I was playing cards with my husband when he dared me to kill him as he wanted to die. I picked up a mallet, and he said 'You have not the guts to do it'. I then hit him with the mallet. Did you say that? . . . Mrs. Rattenbury, please pay attention.

ALMA. Yes. I'm sorry. What?

O'CONNOR. Did you say that to Inspector Mills?

ALMA. Yes.

O'CONNOR. You remember saying every word?

ALMA. Yes.

O'CONNOR. In spite of having consumed the best part of a bottle of whiskey?

ALMA. My mind was perfectly clear.

O'CONNOR. Perfectly clear? Half an hour before you signed that you were playing the gramophone full blast, dancing about the room half dressed, and trying to kiss several of the police-men—

ALMA. Oh dear! Was I really? They didn't say that at the Magistrates' Court.

O'CONNOR. No, because it didn't suit their case. But they'll say it at the trial because it'll suit mine.

ALMA. Oh . . . Must you? . . . Dancing about half naked, and—
She covers her face and shoulders.

—Oh dear! How could I have!

O'CONNOR. You mean you don't remember doing that?

ALMA. No. Nothing like that at all. Just a lot of noise and people there, and me trying to forget and—oh how awful! Oh, I couldn't have—

O'CONNOR. This has come to you as a complete surprise.

ALMA. Oh yes—

O'CONNOR. And yet you remember *clearly every word* of a statement you made only half an hour later, when according to the police you had had even more to drink? . . . Mrs. Rattenbury!

ALMA *looks up at him, realising she is caught.*

ALMA. *(at length)* My mind must have cleared.

O'CONNOR. And you'll say that in court?

ALMA. I certainly will.

O'CONNOR. Right. Where did you find this mallet?
Pause.

ALMA. Lying about.

O'CONNOR. In the sitting-room?

ALMA. No. It couldn't have been, could it? It must have been in the hall.

O'CONNOR. Did you know that Wood had borrowed it from his father earlier that evening?

ALMA. No.

O'CONNOR. What did you do with the mallet afterwards?

ALMA. I hid it.

O'CONNOR. Why?

ALMA *hesitates.*

If you were going to confess, why did you hide it?

ALMA. It looked so horrible.

O'CONNOR. More horrible than the body of your husband with his head caved in?

ALMA. *(with a half scream)* Don't—

O'CONNOR. I must. *Where* did you hide it, Mrs. Rattenbury?

ALMA. I can't remember, even now.

O'CONNOR. Why should Wood know where the mallet was, and not you?

24

ALMA. He didn't know.

O'CONNOR. He did. On his arrest, two days after yours, he described to the police exactly where he had hidden it in the garden. And exactly there they found it—with his fingerprints all over it.

ALMA. Well, they would be. He'd carried it all the way from his father's.

O'CONNOR. And why weren't yours on it?

Pause.

ALMA. I wore gloves.

O'CONNOR. Where did you find the gloves?

ALMA. Oh I have them upstairs. Lots of pairs.

Pause.

O'CONNOR. Your story then is this: Your husband asks you to kill him. You agree. You go out into the hall to find a suitable implement, and find a gardener's mallet, borrowed that evening by Wood. You leave it there, go upstairs and choose a pair of gloves. You come downstairs, pick up the mallet in your gloved hands and hit your husband three times on the back of the head—the *back* of the head, Mrs. Rattenbury, not the front—

ALMA. Don't—don't—

O'CONNOR. And kill him. You then hide the mallet somewhere in the garden, but you can't remember where, and presumably you put the gloves back in a drawer of your bedroom. You then ring up the police, to whom you give a full confession.

ALMA *is silent. She is trapped and knows it.*

Mrs. Rattenbury, if I told that story in court, the jury's laughter would drown my voice.

ALMA. *(indifferent)* Well, if they don't believe it, that's that.

O'CONNOR. No, it isn't quite that, Mrs. Rattenbury. If I tell that story in court, do you know what the jury will believe, they will believe that it was Wood who killed your husband, with a mallet specially acquired for precisely that purpose, and that he did so with your knowledge and your consent, certainly under your influence, and very probably at your urging. That will make you both equally guilty of murder, and your efforts to shield Wood will have the effect of putting a noose around his neck just as surely as around your own.

ALMA. You're just trying to scare me. If I say I did it alone, how can they find *him* guilty?

25

O'CONNOR. They can and they will. Mrs. Rattenbury, would you like to tell us the truth?

ALMA, *struggling to keep her composure, finds it hard to reply. But when she does her voice is firm and unwavering.*

ALMA. I've already told you. I killed Ratz alone and George had nothing to do with it.

Pause. O'CONNOR *stares at her steadily, then begins to put his papers together.*

O'CONNOR. Montagu—it seems there is nothing more.

MONTAGU. Mr. O'Connor. Might I—?

O'CONNOR. By all means.

He continues to gather his papers. MONTAGU *leans forward with a smile.*

MONTAGU. Mrs. Rattenbury, we've come to know each other quite well in the last few weeks, haven't we?

ALMA. Oh yes, very well.

MONTAGU. During our talks, one of those things I've found out about you is that you're a very affectionate person. I mean, for instance, you told me how much you like that wardress—

ALMA. Phyllis? Oh yes. She's a dear.

MONTAGU. And Irene Riggs.

ALMA. I love Irene.

MONTAGU. Then you've told me often how fond you were of your husband.

ALMA. Old Ratz? (*Sincerely*) Yes. He was a funny old thing in his way, but I *was* fond of him. Very fond of him really.

MONTAGU. (gently) Mrs. Rattenbury, how can you possibly expect *me*—to believe that you deliberately hit him with a garden mallet with such force that his blood gushed out on the carpet—

ALMA. Stop . . .

MONTAGU. —at the first stroke, that you shattered his skull with the second—

ALMA. (*jumping up*) Stop it, stop it!

MONTAGU. —opening up his head so that his brains were exposed—

ALMA. (*screaming*) No, no, no! Stop it!

She puts her hands over her ears. MONTAGU *continues inexorably.*

MONTAGU. That you changed the grip on the mallet and hit him on the right side of his head opening up a gash just over the eye from which the blood spurted half across the room, and would have blinded him helplessly if he'd stayed alive—

ALMA *hands to her ears, is now sobbing helplessly.*

—and that you coldly left him there in that chair to die suffocating in his own blood—while you calmly hid the mallet in the garden, and the gloves upstairs.

Helpless with sobs she has tried now to get away from him as far as she can but he comes up to her.

How can you expect me to believe that you, of all people, did that to him.

Moaning, she makes no reply. With a brusque gesture he pulls her hands from her ears.

Above all how can you go on loving and shielding the man who did?

She falls into a chair, sobbing. He puts his hand gently on her shoulder.

He joins O'CONNOR, *who has been watching the scene dispassionately, except for a faint annoyance that it was his Junior and not himself that achieved the breakthrough.*

He presses a bell.

O'CONNOR. (*in what he plainly thinks is an inaudible murmur*) Yes. That was quite good work, Montagu.

JOAN *comes in.*

MONTAGU. We're going, wardress.

JOAN. Yes, sir. On your feet, Rattenbury.

MONTAGU. No, no. Let her sit for a moment.

JOAN. (*understanding the reason*) Yes, sir.

MONTAGU. Please try and save your life, Mrs. Rattenbury, believe me, I think it's worth saving.

JOAN *goes off with the two lawyers.*

O'CONNOR (*off*) But it's just a matter of timing, you see. A breakthrough of that kind is of little moment unless one can follow it up at once. And that of course—after you, my dear fellow—you were quite unable to do.

We hear a door clang, then JOAN *comes back.* ALMA's *tears have nearly stopped, but it is plain that her small handkerchief has become a soggy ball.* JOAN *watches her for a moment in silence then reaches for the 'soggy ball' and substitutes for it a massive but serviceable handkerchief of her own.*

ALMA. (*seated*) Ta.

She wipes her eyes and face, offers the handkerchief back to JOAN.

JOAN. Keep it.

ALMA. Thank you, love. Thank you, Wardress Webster.

She stuffs the vast napkin into her bag and stands up. JOAN *pushes her roughly back again. Then, after a lot of fumbling, she produces a packet of cigarettes and proffers it.*

JOAN. (*at length*) What is it?

ALMA. Nothing. They're trying to get me to say something and I won't, that's all.

JOAN. They usually know best.

ALMA. Not in this case. In this case I know best. You see, Wardress Webster—

JOAN. Joan—

ALMA. Well you see, Joan, they both seemed to think just now that I didn't want to save my life—as if anyone in the world doesn't want to save their life—me above all others. I love life—I always have.

JOAN *nods sympathetically.*

It's just the cost, you see—

She could be speaking about the price of a length of crêpe de chine. JOAN *nods sympathetically however, as if she understood. The lights fade.*

The lights come up on the sitting-room.

STELLA. Is anything the matter, Tony?

TONY. No, nothing!

STELLA. Nervous?

MRS. DAVENPORT. Petrified.

STELLA. I heard on the wireless there's an enormous crowd already, and they're getting out mounted police for tomorrow. 'Fears for the female prisoner's safety' or something . . . I suppose you're sure you'll be in Court Number One?

MRS. DAVENPORT. Yes. 'Fraid so.

STELLA. Have you got your speech ready?

MRS. DAVENPORT. I know what I'm going to say. I can't judge this woman fairly and no power on earth can make me.

STELLA. Are you sure you wouldn't like a coffee?

MRS. DAVENPORT. Oh, all right, yes.

STELLA. It's very sweet of you to have these qualms but if I were you I'd go in there, play noughts and crosses for 4 or 5 days, and then vote guilty with the eleven others. *She goes out.*

MRS. DAVENPORT. Tony, what's the matter with you?

TONY. Nothing.

28

Pause.

MRS. DAVENPORT. I know what it is.

TONY. *(startled)* What?

MRS. DAVENPORT. You've written to Irene Dunne, and she hasn't answered.

TONY *doesn't reply.* MRS. DAVENPORT *gets up to go to the door.*

TONY. Mum—I want to see Dad.

MRS. DAVENPORT. You can't—without my permission.

TONY. I want your permission.

Pause.

MRS. DAVENPORT. When?

TONY. Now. Tonight.

MRS. DAVENPORT. Certainly not.

TONY. I have to see him. I have to. It's a matter of life and death—

MRS. DAVENPORT. Don't be absurd.

TONY. I meant that literally Mum. Life and death. What's more, whether I get your permission or not, I'm going to see him— now, if he's in. If he's not I'll wait until he is.

Pause.

MRS. DAVENPORT. What happened?

TONY. I can't tell you.

Pause.

MRS. DAVENPORT. There's nothing you can't tell me. Whatever it is, Tony, you've got to tell me.

TONY. I'd sooner die.

MRS. DAVENPORT. *(trying to make light of it)* And I suppose you mean *that* literally too?

TONY. Yes! I'm sorry, Mum, but it's something that can only be talked about between men.

Pause.

MRS. DAVENPORT. When did you become a man?

TONY. Do you remember the evening I was reading about Mrs. Rattenbury and you took the paper away from me?

Pause.

MRS. DAVENPORT. Yes. Very clearly. It was the evening you went to the Kensington with Randolph.

TONY. Yes. Only I didn't go to the cinema. I went—somewhere else—on my own—don't blame Randy. He warned me—he didn't want me to go—

MRS. DAVENPORT *is silent and unmoving.*

29

I'm sorry, but that's all I can tell you.

MRS. DAVENPORT. No, it isn't. A boy should be able to tell his mother *everything*.

TONY. I'm not a boy any longer, Mum. I'm grown up . . . A pretty horrible way to grow up, I know—but it's happened, and there it is . . . I went to a doctor and I know what I've got to face now.

MRS. DAVENPORT. Who is this doctor?

TONY. Oh, anonymous. I'm anonymous too. Someone at St. George's hospital. There's a notice up in lavatories in Tube Stations telling you where to go. I didn't have the courage until today.

MRS. DAVENPORT. You should have seen Doctor Macintyre—

TONY. And have him tell you?

MRS. DAVENPORT. *You've* told me.

TONY. Not the lot. Not the sordid details. Not the things I've got to do in the bathroom twice a day. But not in *this* bathroom—I'm determined on that.

MRS. DAVENPORT. (*bravely*) Why *not* this bathroom?
TONY *smiles and shakes his head.*
. . . I won't say a word to you about it. I promise you . . . If it's not serious, if it's just something you'll get over with treatment—

TONY. Mum—twice a day for maybe six weeks, maybe longer, I'll have to lock myself in there—(*He points off*)—and you'll hear a tap running. Do you honestly think I can hope to come out of there without knowing what you're saying to yourself: 'My son has committed a filthy, disgusting act, and he's been punished for it with a filthy, disgusting disease and a filthy, disgusting treatment—'

MRS. DAVENPORT (*roused*) Well, isn't that true?

TONY. No. What I did that night was silly, if you like, but the act was as natural as breathing—and a good deal more pleasant. Goodnight, Mum.

MRS. DAVENPORT. Tony, don't you realise what I've got to go through tomorrow? You're not going to him now. I won't allow it.

TONY. What will you do? Get out a warrant? And have me tell the judge about my adventure in Paddington? I'm sorry, Mum. I *am* terribly sorry. (*He goes to the door*) Don't wait up. If he'll have me, I'll stay the night.

He goes out. MRS. DAVENPORT *is motionless for a moment—then suddenly she shudders—quite violently, as if she were ill.*

STELLA. (*coming in*) Where's Tony?

MRS. DAVENPORT (*incoherently muttering*) That . . . that . . . woman.

THE LIGHTS FADE.

Cries of 'Kill her!' 'Hang her!' *Odd screams of* 'Hanging's too good for her! Give her the Cat too!' *can also be heard. Interspersed with barked orders from the police, and over all the sound of an incensed woman* (JOAN) *as she roars abuse at the crowd.*

JOAN. (*off*) Out of the way, you old bitch, or I'll fetch you one in the crutch— . . . You, you bastard, call yourself a man? Bash 'em, officer! . . . What's your baton for? Hit that old cow on the conk—that's more like it! Push, push! Run, dear, run.

The lights have dimly lit a cell. A woman, seemingly a wardress, runs inside and cowers in the corner. We do not see her face.

(*off*) Get that door closed, officer!

A door clangs and there is comparative silence.

(*off*) Bloody morons—the lot of 'em.

She comes into the cell and turns on the light simultaneously. We see she has made a gallant attempt to dress as MRS. RATTENBURY *might be expected to—with pretty femininity, and a decorative hat. What now spoils the effect is that the hat is over one eye, her dress is torn nearly off her and she has an incipient black eye.*

(*cheerfully*) Well dear, that worked a treat, didn't it?

The huddled figure in wardress uniform reveals herself to be a very scared and bewildered ALMA.

There's no better weapon than a lady's handbag I always say—

She drops it on to a table whence it emits a sharp sound.

Come on now. Get out of that uniform. Your dress is here.

She throws dress down on table.

ALMA. They were shouting: 'Kill her!'

JOAN. You mustn't take any notice, dear. There are a lot of ill people in the world. Far more than anyone knows. Have a cup of coffee.

Out of the bag (which also contains a brick) she brings a thermos.

31

ALMA. Joan—

JOAN. Yes, dear?

ALMA. Why?

JOAN. God knows. I've seen it often before. Never as bad as this, I grant, but—envy, that's what I think it is—plain envy.

ALMA. How can they envy me now?

JOAN. Well, you in the Old Bailey, centre of attention . . . But of course, now it's hate—mob hate, which is the nastiest, illest, ugliest thing in the whole world . . . Mind you, I'm not the Pope. Let's get changed, dear. I don't want the lawyers to catch us like this.

ALMA. (*hands to her face*) Hatred is awful!

JOAN. Forget them! It's a compliment to be hated by them. (*Spreading out the dress*) There's the dress you wanted— You're going to look a picture in court, I know it—

The lights fade as they both dress, coming up immediately on the lawyer's robing room. Some lockers and a bench are all that is necessary. CASSWELL *is finishing robing himself as* O'CONNOR *comes in.*

O'CONNOR. Ah, Casswell, just the man I want to see. Is the enemy about?

CASSWELL. Croom-Johnson? He's just left to muster his witnesses.

O'CONNOR. And quite a crowd he's got, I gather. Was he looking cocky?

CASSWELL. (*gloomily*) He's every reason to, hasn't he?

O'CONNOR. We'll see. How's your lad?

CASSWELL. Wood? I haven't seen him yet today.

O'CONNOR. Very spirited disposition, I hear.

CASSWELL. That's one word for it. I call it cheeky. Cheeky and stubborn.

O'CONNOR. A bad combination. How far are you involving us in the borrowing of the mallet?

CASSWELL. Wood's father is going to say he assumed the boy was borrowing it with your client's knowledge and consent!

O'CONNOR. Assumption is nothing. I can tear that apart. What exactly did he tell the father he was borrowing it for?

CASSWELL. To put up a sun-shelter. In the garden.

O'CONNOR. A sun-shelter? In mid-March, and on one of the coldest days of the year?

CASSWELL. Was it?

32

O'CONNOR. Yes.

CASSWELL. Should I have known that? Is it important?

O'CONNOR. It is to me.

CASSWELL. Why?

O'CONNOR. Trade secret, dear boy. If I thought it would help you I'd tell you—but it won't.

CASSWELL. (*suspiciously*) You look cheerful.

O'CONNOR. I always look cheerful. It's half the battle. You'd better do something about yourself. Try a little rouge or something.

CASSWELL. (*looking at himself*) I didn't sleep at all last night.

O'CONNOR. That's a mistake. I had a large dinner at the Garrick, got away from the bloody actors and slept two hours in the smoking room. After that—home and bed. Now listen, Casswell, I don't want to bully, but any suggestion that we wielded that mallet and I shall not hesitate to remind the jury that while we are a poor weak woman who couldn't drive an iron peg into soft peat in under forty whacks, you are a hulking great muscular brute of an ex-builder who can easily knock a man's head off in three.

CASSWELL. (*with resigned sigh*) Yes. And did.

O'CONNOR. That's right. And did. You're not disputing your statement of confession to the police on the day of your arrest?

CASSWELL. How can I?

O'CONNOR. I don't know. I only know I'm disputing every one of mine. After half an hour in there with the Bournemouth Constabulary those seven separate confessions will be floating down past Croom-Johnson's nose like confetti. I suppose while you were knocking the old man's block in, we were winding up the gramophone and cheering and egging you on—?

CASSWELL. Of course. I'm sorry, O'Connor, but it's my only chance.

O'CONNOR. Of what.

CASSWELL. Of getting a manslaughter.

O'CONNOR *chuckles.*

I'd better warn you I intend to push your evil moral influence and your shameless depravity as hard as I can.

O'CONNOR. Push away, my dear fellow, push away, if it's all you've got, I'm going to push your psycho-pathological rages, your surliness and your fits of sudden violence. You won't mind that, I hope?

CASSWELL. The reverse. It might help me to a guilty but insane.

O'CONNOR. Under Humphreys? Not a hope. He sleeps with the Macnaghten rules under his pillow. Did the murderer know what he was doing at the time that he did it? If he did, did he know that what he was doing was wrong? (*He helps himself into a pair of slippers*) I'd say that your boy had a teeny inkling of both.

CASSWELL. Do you always wear slippers in court?

O'CONNOR. Always. Because they make us as uncomfortable as they can up here (*he indicates his upper half*) is no reason why we shouldn't be cosy down here. Anyway, aren't you supposed to have committed the murder under the influence of a lorry load of cocaine?

CASSWELL. Yes, damn it. He would choose the one drug that heightens the perceptions rather than dulling them.

O'CONNOR. Change your drug.

CASSWELL. I can't. Cocaine is what I'm instructed to take, and as a Poor Persons' Defence Act Lawyer, I've got to obey my instructions.

O'CONNOR. (*sententiously*) My dear fellow, we all have to obey our instructions. Some of us sometimes manage to get them just a little bit—confused—

CASSWELL. Not a chance here. He won't budge an inch.

O'CONNOR. Where did you get the cocaine from?

CASSWELL. Someone somewhere in London. We can't remember who or where.

O'CONNOR. Good God. And you're stuck with his whole confession?

CASSWELL. No way round it. (*Gloomily swallows two pills*)

O'CONNOR. Hangover?

CASSWELL. No. Nerves. Does one ever get over them?

O'CONNOR. Never. They get worse with age.

CASSWELL. I've never seen you look even remotely nervous.

O'CONNOR. Ah. That's something we do learn—never to show it. But that carafe I always have in front of me. You don't think that's plain water, do you?

CASSWELL. Gin?

O'CONNOR. Vodka. Safe as houses. Not a whiff from a foot away. Is this your first capital charge?

CASSWELL. No. But with the others I had some chance—

O'CONNOR. My dear boy, while there's life there's hope.

CASSWELL. Our hope—their lives.

Pause. O'CONNOR *turns slowly on him.*

O'CONNOR. Do you think there's a single moment I'm unconscious of that?

CASSWELL. No. Well, I'd better have one last shot at getting him to change his drug into something else.

O'CONNOR. Yes. Good luck. (*Suddenly savage*) But look, Casswell!

CASSWELL *turns.*

If there's the faintest suggestion that he got any drugs from her, I'll be on you like a tiger. That poor bitch has got enough to carry into the court without dope peddling (*His hand on* CASSWELL'S *arm*) Get him to come off drugs altogether. Use our shameless depravity and pernicious influence. It's much safer. And I can't hit back. That's my honest advice, old man.

CASSWELL. (*with a sigh*) Well, it would be a very foolish advocate who neglected advice from such a source. Thank you.

O'CONNOR. You're very welcome.

CASSWELL *is on his way out when a thought strikes him.*

CASSWELL. Unless such a source happened to be fighting the same trial with him.

O'CONNOR. As an ally, dear fellow—

CASSWELL. An ally who wouldn't hesitate to slash my throat if he thought it could help his client.

O'CONNOR. Slash your throat, my dear Casswell, I've just given you an open invitation to attack me in my weakest spot, to wit, my deplorable moral character. Now how could that possibly be slashing your throat?

MONTAGU *comes in.*

Ah, Montagu. Good . . . (*With an innocent smile*) Have you got our friend in all right?

The lights fade on O'CONNOR *and* MONTAGU *and stay on* CASSWELL *as he walks unhappily towards a small cell where the lights come on to show* WOOD *sitting patiently.* O'CONNOR *and* MONTAGU—*who is already gowned—disappear from view.*

CASSWELL. (*calls*) Warder!

WOOD. (*chirpily*) Morning, Mr. Casswell. Did you hear that crowd cheering me when I arrived? Some of them shouted 'Good luck, lad'—and 'we won't let you swing'—things like that . . .

CASSWELL. Mr. Wood, we have only a few minutes before you go on trial for your life. Are you still determined to instruct

35

me that you murdered Rattenbury when under the influence of cocaine?

Pause.

WOOD. Perce Wood, the odd job boy, has come a long way, hasn't he, instructing someone dressed up like you . . . Well, I instruct you, Mr. Casswell, I done the old man in when I was crazed from cocaine and not responsible for my actions. And that's what I'm going to tell them.

CASSWELL. You won't have the opportunity. I am not putting you in the witness box.

WOOD. How can you stop me?

CASSWELL. By not calling you.

WOOD. Why not? You've got to!

CASSWELL. I am not putting you into the witness box because I would not like to hear you explaining to Mr. Croom-Johnson, one of the most devastating cross-examiners at the Bar, exactly how you became 'a dope fiend'.

WOOD. But that's my defence!

CASSWELL. What does cocaine look like? Mr. Wood? I mean, what colour is it?

WOOD. Colour? (*After a pause*) Brown.

CASSWELL. Brown.

WOOD. With black specks.

CASSWELL. With black specks . . . And if you went into the witness box you would tell Mr. Croom-Johnson that?

WOOD. Of course.

CASSWELL. And if he asked you why, in popular parlance, it was called snow, how would you answer him?

WOOD. I don't know—I didn't know it was.

CASSWELL. It is called snow because it is white, Mr. Wood—the purest possible *white*.

Pause.

WOOD. Jesus.

CASSWELL. Exactly.

WOOD. But without cocaine where's my defence?

CASSWELL. I've told you—many times.

Pause.

WOOD. (*violently*) No!

CASSWELL. You are of age to be hanged, Mr. Wood.

WOOD. I know.

CASSWELL. You are disposed then to die?

36

WOOD. No, I'm not. I want to live—Christ, don't I want to live. But I'm not going to say *she* made me do it. They can tear me apart before they'll get me to say that.

CASSWELL. I don't think you quite understand—

WOOD. (*violently*) It's you who don't bloody understand. Alma Rattenbury, sex-mad drunken bloody cow that she is, lying deceitful bitch to come to that—she's the only woman I've ever had, and the only one I've ever loved, and I'm not going to shop her now . . . No, it's you who don't bloody understand, Mr. Casswell, nor the others either.

Pause.

CASSWELL. Very likely. I'll see you in court.

CASSWELL *picks up his brief. The* lights *fade, coming up immediately on the other cell.* ALMA *is now dressed.*

JOAN. Not long now, dear. I said you'd look a treat.

O'CONNOR *and* MONTAGU *come in gowned, and carrying their wigs.*

O'CONNOR. Wardress—bring Mrs. Rattenbury, please.

JOAN. Sir.

MONTAGU. (*to* ALMA) I hope they didn't upset you too much outside.

ALMA. Well, it came as rather a shock

O'CONNOR. Mrs. Rattenbury, it is my duty to tell you that there will be deep prejudice against you up there.

ALMA. Oh, I know.

O'CONNOR. Very deep indeed, I'm afraid. You must be prepared to answer some very venomous questions.

ALMA. (*simply*) Oh, but I'm not going to answer any questions. I'm not going into the witness box. I told you that, Mr. Montagu.

Pause. O'CONNOR *makes a sign to* MONTAGU *who slips out of the room.*

O'CONNOR. I beg you most earnestly to reconsider, Madam.

ALMA. I'm sorry. I can't. I will not go into the witness box. *Not* under oath. *Not* giving George away . . .

O'CONNOR. Because you want him to see you as a tragic heroine? You love him as much as that?

ALMA. Me a heroine to George? . . . That's funny. To him I'm just a drunken sexy lying bitch. He's told me so a million times.

O'CONNOR. Then why in Heaven's name sacrifice yourself for him?

37

ALMA. Because it's right. I'm *responsible*, and neither you nor anyone . . .

MONTAGU *brings* CHRISTOPHER *in.*

CHRISTOPHER. Hello, Mummy.

ALMA *stands still for a moment, then turns furiously on* O'CONNOR.

ALMA. What kind of a man are you?

O'CONNOR. A humane man, Mrs. Rattenbury. I thought you might like a couple of minutes with your boy before you go into court . . . (*With a curt beckoning nod he ushers* MONTAGU *out, following him.*

CHRISTOPHER. What's Mr. O'Connor done, Mummy? What's made you angry with him?

ALMA. Never mind. (*She embraces him*) How are you, Chris?

CHRISTOPHER. Oh all right.

ALMA. They brought you up from school?

CHRISTOPHER. I wanted to come. (*Looking at her*) You're in an ordinary dress . . .

ALMA. Yes. Do you like it?

CHRISTOPHER. Yes. It's nice. I thought—

ALMA. That I'd be in stripes and arrows? Not yet.

CHRISTOPHER. What's it like in prison?

ALMA. Oh, it's not really prison. And the wardresses—the people I'm with—they're very nice. (*Suddenly clutching him*) They didn't bring you through those crowds?

CHRISTOPHER. Oh yes—but nobody knew who *I* was. They were nasty people, though.

ALMA. Did you hear them shouting?

CHRISTOPHER. (*quickly*) Oh, I didn't listen, Mummy.

She clutches him fiercely again, then lets him go.

ALMA. And how's little John?

CHRISTOPHER. Oh all right. He gets a bit tearful, sometimes.

ALMA. They haven't told him—

CHRISTOPHER. Oh no.

ALMA. He misses me?

CHRISTOPHER. *Misses* you?

Pause.

ALMA. (*trying to steady her voice*) Well Chris, what have you been told to say to me?

CHRISTOPHER. (*bewildered*) Told to say to you?

ALMA. By Mr. O'Connor?

CHRISTOPHER. Nothing.

ALMA. Really? Nothing?

CHRISTOPHER. Well, the obvious thing, of course.

ALMA. What's that?

CHRISTOPHER. About your not giving George away in court. It was a bit of a shock, because he says the jury may find you guilty: but he put it so nicely though . . .

ALMA. *(faintly)* How did he put it?

CHRISTOPHER. Well he said that as a schoolboy I'd understand about not sneaking on a friend . . . Well of course I understand except in this kind of thing . . . I mean in a case of murder— real murder—what they might do—except, of course, they'd never do that to you . . . Oh Mummy! . . .

He runs to her. She clasps him firmly and allows him to cry on her breast.

Oh damn! I promised I wouldn't.

ALMA. *(at length)* What else did Mr. O'Connor put so nicely?

CHRISTOPHER. He said that as I was nearly grown-up I should understand that when a woman has a choice between her lover and her children she's almost bound to put her lover first.

ALMA, *apparently unmoved and unmoving, looks down at his head.*

O'CONNOR *and* MONTAGU *come back.* ALMA *has not moved.*

O'CONNOR. The judge has sent us his signal. *(He puts his arm on* CHRISTOPHER'S *shoulder)* You should be getting to your seat, young man. A Mr. Watson, outside, will be sitting with you—

ALMA. *(appalled)* Christopher's not going to be in court?

O'CONNOR. Of course.

ALMA. Will he be there every day?

O'CONNOR. That depends. Say au revoir to your mother, old chap.

CHRISTOPHER. Goodbye, Mummy. Good luck.

O'CONNOR. Montagu, you take him to Watson—Wardress!

ALMA *lets* CHRISTOPHER *kiss her, patting him absently on the head as he goes. He goes out with* MONTAGU.

ALMA. *(at length)* Don't think you've won, Mr. O'Connor.

O'CONNOR. Oh I never think that about any case, until the end.

ACT TWO

As at the beginning of Act One, the lights *come up on* ALMA *and*
MRS. DAVENPORT.
A light then comes up on the JUDGE.

JUDGE. Mrs.—er—Davenport, I understand from the Jury Bailiff
that you wish to be excused from jury service on the grounds
of conscience?

MRS. DAVENPORT. Yes. From this particular jury, on this
particular case. I will serve on any other.

JUDGE. You have a conscientious objection to capital punish-
ment?

MRS. DAVENPORT. No, My Lord.

JUDGE. Where then does your conscience enter the matter?

MRS. DAVENPORT. My Lord, I have a deep prejudice against that
woman. (*She acknowledges the dock*)

JUDGE. The female prisoner?

MRS. DAVENPORT. Yes.

JUDGE. Would the female prisoner please rise?

ALMA *rises. She stares at* MRS. DAVENPORT *without surprise—
even with faint understanding.*

Do you know this woman personally?

MRS. DAVENPORT. No, but it's as if I did.

JUDGE. I don't follow, I'm afraid.

MRS. DAVENPORT. I've read about her in the newspapers.

Pause.

JUDGE. Is that all?

The lights come up dimly on the Lawyers.

MRS. DAVENPORT. My Lord, you are here to see that this woman
gets a fair trial. Isn't that so?

JUDGE. It is, Madam. It is also my duty, as it will be yours, to
put out of my head all of the deplorably wide publicity this
case has attracted, and to allow the facts of the case—

MRS. DAVENPORT. I am sorry, My Lord. I know these arguments.
You see I know about the law. My father was a judge in
India—

JUDGE. Mrs.—er—but I don't—

MRS. DAVENPORT (*passionately*) I warn you now, and I warn
these gentlemen who are defending her that no matter what
oath I am forced to take, I will not be able to try this woman's
case without deep prejudice. My mind is set against her.

Pause. Her sincerity has evidently impressed the JUDGE. *He frowns*

43

thoughtfully and then addresses the LAWYERS' *bench. As he does so, the* lights *fade except on* ALMA *and* MRS. DAVENPORT. *The discussion between the* JUDGE *and the* LAWYERS *is only dimly heard.*

JUDGE. Mr. O'Connor, you have heard my view. It remains unaltered. However you might have cause for a challenge 'propter affectum'. If you have I am very willing to hear it.

O'CONNOR. If Your Lordship permits?

The JUDGE *nods.* O'CONNOR *talks to* MONTAGU *in a low voice, their backs to the Judge.*

MONTAGU. She's an asset.

O'CONNOR. On the question of bias?

MONTAGU. Exactly. You can refer to her in your final address.

He rises again.

O'CONNOR. My Lord, we will not challenge.

CASSWELL. No challenge, My Lord. The prejudice does not appear to be directed against my client.

JUDGE. Obviously, Mr. Croom-Johnson, you won't wish to challenge. But do you think I am right?

CROOM-JOHNSON, *prosecuting counsel, gets up.*

CROOM-JOHNSON. I feel Your Lordship's view of the matter is both wise and just.

The light *comes up on the* JUDGE.

JUDGE. Mrs.Davenport, we all find that there are no grounds for your self-disqualification. Will you then take the oath?

CLERK. Take the book in your right hand and repeat the words on the cards.

The lights *fade on the* JUDGE *and the* LAWYERS.

Now only the TWO WOMEN *can be seen facing each other across the courtroom.*

MRS. DAVENPORT. (*solemnly, after a pause, the bible in her right hand, a card in the other*) I, do solemnly swear by Almighty God that I will well and truly try the issues between our Sovereign Lord the King and the prisoners at the bar and will give a true verdict according to the evidence.

The lights *fade quickly to* BLACKOUT.

In the sitting-room, STELLA *is dimly seen reading a newspaper. The* lights *come up on Court Number One at the Old Bailey. The court is not in session. The lawyers are chatting.*

CASSWELL. (*to* CROOM-JOHNSON) Congratulations on your opening.

CROOM-JOHNSON. Oh, thank you, Casswell, thank you.

CASSWELL. Admirably fair, I thought.

CROOM-JOHNSON. I'm glad.

O'CONNOR. (*muttering some distance away, to* MONTAGU) Fair! If that bloody Croom-Johnson uses the phrase 'Woman and *boy*' once more, I'm going to have him disbarred and demand a re-trial—

MONTAGU. Why don't you tell him?

O'CONNOR. And let him know he's scored? We'll have 'woman and *child*' then . . .

CROOM-JOHNSON *moves near.*

(*Calling*) Good opening, Croom-Johnson.

CROOM-JOHNSON. Thank you. It was, fair, I think.

O'CONNOR. Every bit as fair as we've come to expect of you.

CROOM-JOHNSON. How kind. Extraordinary incident that was— that woman juror saying she was prejudiced against your client. Very distressing to hear that kind of thing, you know. I wonder you didn't challenge.

O'CONNOR. Yes. I suppose I should have done—

CROOM-JOHNSON. (*suspiciously*) You won't, of course, be able to make any reference to her in your final address—

O'CONNOR. Oh no. That would be most deeply improper.

CROOM-JOHNSON. Well I honestly think my opening will have helped remove some of her prejudices—

O'CONNOR. Yes.

CROOM-JOHNSON. I emphasised that this was in no way a court of morals—and that they were to direct their attention only to the facts of the case.

O'CONNOR. (*unable to contain himself*)—brought against 'this woman and this boy'—

CROOM-JOHNSON. Ah. I did notice your uneasiness at the appellation 'boy'. But what else in all honesty could I call him, O'Connor? The jury have only to look at the dock—

O'CONNOR. —and see a hulking young man, old enough to be hanged and a woman young-looking enough to pass herself off successfully as his sister.

CROOM-JOHNSON. But the gap in ages is so much a part of the case. One must steel oneself, must one not, to face facts, however disagreeable. (*He gathers up his papers*)

O'CONNOR. Bloody man!—Do you know I drew him in the Bar golf tournament, and he wouldn't give me a fourteen inch putt? . . . I missed it too. I've got to beat that bugger—(*He smiles at* CROOM-JOHNSON *as he passes again*)—if it's the last thing I do.

As the lawyers leave the court, the lights fade, coming up as MRS. DAVENPORT *enters wearily.* STELLA, *lying on a sofa, is reading an evening newspaper.*

MRS. DAVENPORT. Has Tony come home?

STELLA. Tony? No.

MRS. DAVENPORT. Oh, God, I won't let John take him away from me, I won't, I won't. (*She sits on sofa*)

STELLA. Darling, you've had a tiring day. Do you want a cup of tea?

MRS. DAVENPORT. No, but I'd love a drink. A whiskey.

STELLA. That's bold of you. (*She gets up to pour the whiskey*) So it didn't work this morning?

MRS. DAVENPORT. No. And what's worse the jury has elected me forewoman because I'd let out that father was a judge.

STELLA. My dear, how too splendid. What d'you have in court tomorrow?

MRS. DAVENPORT. The rest of the prosecution witnesses, I think. Oh, Stella, it's all so foul.

She goes out to the bedroom. STELLA *picks up her newspaper and crosses to the phone.*

STELLA (*calling*) Darling, do you know what odds the bookmakers are laying on Mrs. Rattenbury being convicted?

MRS. DAVENPORT (*off*) Odds? How can they be so unfeeling?

STELLA No principles, bookmakers. In the city they're even taking bets on whether she'll hang. Good odds too. But for her being convicted—it's here somewhere. (*She looks in the paper*) Yes, they're giving three to one.

MRS. DAVENPORT (*off*) Only three to one? That woman—it's absurd.

STELLA. Well—if ever I heard a tip straight from the horse's mouth—(*Into receiver*) Hello—still at the office? There's a good Henry! . . . Look, darling, apparently you can get three to one on Mrs. Rattenbury being convicted—well—(*lowering her voice*) Edie's just back from court, and she says that in her view those odds are madly generous . . . Yes, and they've made her forewoman too, so of course she'll have a big say . . . Yes,

a real hot snip. Well, put on six hundred for me, would
you? . . .

TONY *comes in.*

Thank you, darling . . . I will. Henry sends his love. (*She
hangs up*) Tony!

TONY. Hullo, Aunt Stella.

MRS. DAVENPORT *comes in wearing a dressing gown.*

MRS. DAVENPORT. Tony!

TONY. . . . Hullo, Mum.

MRS. DAVENPORT. Tony, thank God. You've come back.

TONY. No, I haven't. Dad's here.

MRS. DAVENPORT. I won't see him!

DAVENPORT *enters.*

I'm not allowed to see you. The Judge said—

DAVENPORT. I remember very well what the Judge said. No
communication of any kind. Hullo, Stella.

STELLA. Hullo, John.

DAVENPORT. So this letter I've brought is just as wrong as my
presence (*He holds out a letter*)

MRS. DAVENPORT. I won't read it.

DAVENPORT. I thought not, which is why I'm delivering it
myself.

STELLA. I'll go.

MRS. DAVENPORT. No don't. Please.

DAVENPORT. I don't mind Stella hearing what I've got to say.
Tony, go down and wait in the car, would you?

MRS. DAVENPORT. Are you taking him away?

DAVENPORT. To the cottage.

MRS. DAVENPORT. And I forbid him to go.

DAVENPORT. Go ahead, Tony.

MRS. DAVENPORT. No—

TONY. Sorry, Mum. Really. I'll call you tomorrow. (*He goes*)

MRS. DAVENPORT. I've only to ring the police—

DAVENPORT. Yes. Then I'd have to give my exact reasons to the
Judge for taking my son away from here. Of course he'd find
the reasons quite insufficient, and I'd be fined or committed,
and Tony would be returned to you. There'd probably be a
little something in the papers, which probably would be read
by Tony's headmaster—

MRS. DAVENPORT. This is pure blackmail.

DAVENPORT. Yes it is, I suppose. It's also a truthful forecast of what would happen, must happen, if you invoke the law.

MRS. DAVENPORT. Exactly what lies have you told his head-master?

DAVENPORT. I told him the truth. Not all of it, but I said the boy had had a severe psychological shock, that he'd attempted suicide—

MRS. DAVENPORT. That's a lie!

DAVENPORT. It's not. The night before last he swallowed some sleeping pills.

MRS. DAVENPORT. No—

DAVENPORT. If you don't believe me, go into the bathroom and look for your sleeping pills. Luckily there were only seven or eight left, and they made him sick at once.

MRS. DAVENPORT. But I'd have heard if—

DAVENPORT. Tony's a polite boy. He can even vomit quietly enough not to wake his mother. And then apparently lie on the bathroom floor, sobbing—but into a towel, quietly.

MRS. DAVENPORT. But is this—thing he has as dreadful as that?

DAVENPORT. Medically it's nothing, provided it's treated promptly . . . It's the psychological shock he won't get over so easily, and he'd never get over it here . . . unless . . .

Pause.

Are you going to read my letter?

MRS. DAVENPORT. Never.

DAVENPORT. Then I'll read it to you. (*He takes the letter and opens it*) 'My dearest Edie—for the sake of Tony, and also for our own sakes, I want you to rescind the decree nisi. It's very easily done, by application to a judge in chambers.

I must tell you with complete truth that there is no other woman in my life. No single other woman, that is. The one you know about left me some months ago, with no regrets on either side. She wasn't important to me. No woman has ever been important to me except yourself. I admit that I've had occasional affairs, but they were necessary to me—you know why—always brief, and usually with a mercenary tinge.

Without you, Edie, and without Tony, I have been a very lonely man. So, I believe, are you lonely without me. Please let me come back into your life. If you do I promise to behave as well as I can. That doesn't, I'm afraid, mean as well as you'd want me to. It can never mean that, Edie my darling, as you know. But if you can only bring yourself to overlook an occasional late night at the office, or the odd dinner at the Club with the Permanent Secretary, I swear a solemn oath to you that you will never otherwise be humiliated. I renounce my conjugal rights entirely, but I earnestly entreat you to let me once again be your loving husband.

John.'

He puts it back in the envelope and hands it to her. She won't take it. He puts it on the coffee table.

MRS. DAVENPORT. Your terms.

DAVENPORT. Yours as well.

MRS. DAVENPORT. The answer is no.

STELLA. Think about it, Edie. For God's sake, think about it.

MRS. DAVENPORT. Stella, how can you? He wants me to—condone adultery? It's unthinkable and you know it. I will not break the standards by which I've lived all my life.

DAVENPORT. Those standards could be wrong, you know. They're certainly becoming a little dated . . . You won't reconsider?

No reply.

Well, I'll say goodbye. (*At the door*) Tell me—this Mrs. Rattenbury, is she for it?

MRS. DAVENPORT. We're not allowed to talk about it.

DAVENPORT. (*smiling*) I don't give much for her chances with you judging her. I don't know anything about Mrs. Rattenbury, except what I've read in the papers, but that's enough to tell me that her vices, which I am sure are deplorable, do add up to some kind of affirmation. Your virtues, Edie, which I know are admirable, add up to precisely nothing. Goodbye!

He goes. MRS. DAVENPORT *picks up the letter, then tears it up decisively. The lights fade as she goes to her room.* STELLA *picks up the pieces of the letter, then sits.*

The Old Bailey. The trial is in its second day, and POLICE SERGEANT BAGWELL *is being examined by* CROOM-JOHNSON *for the prosecution. The dock is unseen.*

CROOM-JOHNSON. At what time did you receive this call from the hospital? You may use your notebook, if there is no objection.

CASSWELL *and the* JUDGE *both nod acceptance.* O'CONNOR *is too busy muttering to* MONTAGU *to notice.*

SERGEANT. The call came through at 2.13 a.m., sir, saying that all attempts to revive the deceased had failed.

49

CROOM-JOHNSON. What did you do then?

SERGEANT. Acting on this information, I duly presented myself at the Villa Madeira, at 2.47 a.m. There was a lot of commotion proceeding from inside—

CROOM-JOHNSON. What kind of commotion?

The lights fade to a spot on the POLICE SERGEANT.

SERGEANT. There was a gramophone playing at full blast, sir— and some female laughter of a shrill nature. There being no answer to the bell I tried the door and found it open. I then entered the sitting-room, and found the female prisoner attired in a nightdress, and two police officers to whom she was making flourishing gestures with her bed jacket—in imitation of bullfighting or some such. I immediately summoned the two officers outside, asked what their business had been, and sent them away. I then proceeded back into the house.

The lights have come up on the sitting-room of the Villa Madeira where ALMA, *dressed as described by the* SERGEANT, *is continuing her cavortings to a now empty room. The gramophone is playing loudly. Suddenly she notices.*

ALMA. Oh damn and blast! (*Plaintively*) Where have you gone? Come back. We're having fun.

She takes a large swig from an evidently almost empty bottle. The record runs out and she goes to change it. She is very drunk. The SERGEANT *comes in, knocking politely at the open door.* ALMA, *at the gramophone, has her back to him.*

SERGEANT. Beg pardon for the intrusion, but would you be—

ALMA. (*with a shriek of joy*) Oh, another lovely policeman! Come in. Come in. We're having a gorgeous time—

The deafening music has started up again.

SERGEANT. (*shouting*) Would you be Mrs. Francis Rattenbury?

ALMA Alma to you, dear. Come and dance—

She puts her arms round his neck. He detaches himself.

SERGEANT. May we have the music down, please?

ALMA. Why? How can we dance with no music?

She tries again to get him to dance. Again he eludes.

SERGEANT. Excuse me, Madam. With your permission?

He goes to the gramophone and turns it off.

ALMA. Oh why did you do that? Now it's quiet. I don't like it quiet—

She goes to the gramophone again. He gently restrains her.

SERGEANT. I'm sorry, Madam, but you could be disturbing the neighbours.

ALMA. (*laughing*) Oh, that's terrible. Disturbing the neighbours is terrible.

SERGEANT. I must ask you again if you are Mrs. Francis Rattenbury?

ALMA. That's right.

SERGEANT. The widow of Francis Rattenbury.

ALMA. Widow?

SERGEANT. You have not been informed of your husband's death?

ALMA. Don't talk about awful things. Let's have some music—

SERGEANT. (*restraining her*) I must ask you, Madam, what you know about your husband's death.

ALMA. Everything. I know everything. (*She shudders and covers her face, then emerges brightly smiling*) I did it, you see. All by myself. All alone. (*Singing and dancing*) All alone, all alone.

She goes to the bottle. The SERGEANT *takes it from her.*

SERGEANT. Who else is in this house?

ALMA. Only Irene.

SERGEANT. Irene?

ALMA. She's my maid. My friend. I sent her up to bed. She knows nothing about it. I want my whiskey—

ALMA *takes the bottle from him. She seems to finish it.*

SERGEANT. And this Irene is the only other person in the house?

ALMA, *in the act of looking for another bottle, stops and turns slowly.*

ALMA. There's George too—

SERGEANT. George?

ALMA. My chauffeur. He's only a boy. He's nothing—just an odd-job-boy—

SERGEANT. Where is he?

ALMA. How would I know? I'm not his mother . . . I expect he's upstairs, asleep. He's very young, you see—

SERGEANT. Madam, I must now caution you. You are not obliged to say anything unless you wish to do so, but whatever you do say will be taken down and may be given in evidence. Do you follow me?

ALMA. Anywhere. Are you married? You've lots of girls I expect—Would you like ten pounds? No, it's a crime to give a policeman money.

SERGEANT. Madam, please.

ALMA. He wanted to die, you see. He said he'd lived too long. He gave me a mallet and dared me to kill him, so I did.

SERGEANT. Where is the mallet?

ALMA. (*yawning*) What?

SERGEANT. The mallet? Where is the mallet?

ALMA. Oh, I'll remember in the morning. (*She gets up*) No, mustn't sleep. I might dream. Let's have that music again—

SERGEANT. (*closing his notebook*) Madam, I propose to telephone the police station, using the callbox outside—

ALMA. There's one in there. Better still there's one in the bedroom.

SERGEANT. I shall use the call-box, thank you, Madam.

ALMA. Please yourself, but you don't know what you're missing—

The SERGEANT *goes out. As he disappears* ALMA *is going towards the gramophone. After he has left she covers her face, emitting a sob, as reality seems to hit her. Then, swaying, she places the record back on the turntable and the music starts up again, deafeningly loud.*

The lights fade *as she moves in time to the music and* come up *on the courtroom. The* SERGEANT *is continuing his evidence. The music overlaps until it too fades out.*

CROOM-JOHNSON. A general question, sergeant, about Mrs. Rattenbury's behaviour. Remembering that only a few hours before, her husband had been brutally killed, how did you react in your mind to her attitude that night?

SERGEANT. I was—disgusted, sir.

CROOM-JOHNSON. In one word, how would you describe her behaviour?

SERGEANT. (*after thought*) Callous. Downright brutal.

CROOM-JOHNSON. Thank you, sergeant.

He sits down.

MONTAGU. Look at the press boys scampering out. Imagine the headlines.

O'CONNOR. They should have waited. (*He rises*) Sergeant, how long have you been in the police force?

SERGEANT. Twenty years, sir.

O'CONNOR. In that time you would, of course, have attended at many gruesome occasions—car accidents and the like?

SERGEANT. Yes, sir. Many.

o'connor. You must then be familiar with the medical phenomenon known as shock?

sergeant. I've seen cases of shock, sir.

o'connor. Severe shock?

sergeant. Some severe.

o'connor. How do such persons usually behave?

sergeant. Well, I'd say, sometimes they're not quite all there.

o'connor. Not quite all there? Not aware of their surroundings, or excited and over-talkative?

sergeant. Both, sir.

o'connor. Inclined to fits either of hysterical weeping or, quite as likely, hysterical laughter—and, generally speaking, inclined to behave entirely out of character?

sergeant. Yes, sir.

o'connor. Why then were you so disgusted at Mrs. Rattenbury's behaviour that night?

sergeant. I didn't think it was shock, sir. I mean I saw no occasion—

o'connor. You saw no occasion? Can you imagine a greater occasion for shock than the brutal murder of a dearly loved husband in her own home? Can you?

sergeant. She didn't seem disturbed, sir. Like I said—she was laughing, and dancing and playing about.

o'connor. (*forcefully*) Good God, man—have you never heard of hysteria?

judge. Mr. O'Connor.

o'connor. I'm sorry, My Lord. Have you never heard of hysteria, Sergeant?

sergeant. Of course, sir.

o'connor. What form does it take?'

sergeant. Laughing, sir. But this wasn't hysterical laughing—

o'connor. And who are you to judge?

sergeant. I've seen hysteria, sir—

o'connor. You've also seen shock, and you failed to recognise that, didn't you? What is the treatment for shock? (*As* sergeant *hesitates*) Come on. You've read your manual. What does it say?

sergeant. One should keep the victim warm, using blankets when obtainable—

o'connor. This victim was half-dressed, on a night in March. Was there a fire in the grate?

53

SERGEANT. No, sir.

O'CONNOR. Were the windows open?

SERGEANT. Yes, sir.

O'CONNOR. Do you remember what the temperature was that night in Bournemouth?

SERGEANT. No, sir. Not exactly.

O'CONNOR. Would it surprise you to learn that at two o'clock on the morning of March 25 the temperature on the town hall roof was recorded as 3 degrees below freezing?

SERGEANT. I remember it was a bit chilly, sir. I didn't know it was as cold as that.

O'CONNOR. It *was* as cold as that. And the windows in the sitting-room were open?

SERGEANT. Yes, sir.

O'CONNOR. Back to the manual. If the victim is *not* kept warm, what does it say can happen to the victim? What is there a danger of?

SERGEANT. Collapse, sir.

O'CONNOR. What happened to Mrs. Rattenbury later that night?

SERGEANT. She did collapse, sir, and had to be put to bed—but that was the whiskey.

O'CONNOR. Was it, indeed? And how much whiskey did Mrs. Rattenbury have to drink that night?

SERGEANT. I don't know, exactly, sir—she was drinking from the bottle, sir—and emptied it.

O'CONNOR. In front of you, sergeant?

SERGEANT. Yes, sir.

O'CONNOR. And you allowed that?

SERGEANT. I had no option, sir.

O'CONNOR. No option? What does your handbook tell you to prevent the victim taking at all costs?'

Pause.

SERGEANT. Alcohol, sir.

O'CONNOR. And why, sergeant? Do you remember why?

Pause.

SERGEANT. (*quoting from memory*) Because the effect of alcohol on a shocked system will greatly increase the symptoms, and will in all respect prove strongly deleterious.

O'CONNOR. And—doesn't it add—sometimes fatal?

SERGEANT. Yes, sir.

O'CONNOR. It may be that you are lucky that in this case it was not. Otherwise you could be facing a very grave charge, sergeant—gross negligence while on duty. That's all.

He sits down. CROOM-JOHNSON *rises.*

CROOM-JOHNSON. Sergeant, has a person in a state of shock ever made sexual advances to you?

SERGEANT. Certainly not, sir.

CROOM-JOHNSON. Or attempted to bribe you?

SERGEANT. No, sir.

CROOM-JOHNSON. Thank you, sergeant.

The SERGEANT *descends from the box.*

That concludes the case for the Crown, My Lord. (*He sits down*)

JUDGE. Mr. O'Connor. Are you ready?

O'CONNOR. Yes, My Lord.

O'CONNOR mutters to MONTAGU, *then shrugs. He rises.*

May it please Your Lordship, members of the Jury, it is my intention to call one witness and one witness only—namely Mrs. Rattenbury. I shall therefore claim the right of the last word—

CROOM-JOHNSON. (*rising swiftly*) My Lord, this sudden manoeuvre of my learned friend puts me at a grave disadvantage.

O'CONNOR. My Lord, I have to confess that I do not know—even at this very second, as I stand here to begin Mrs. Rattenbury's defence, whether she will in fact obey my summons to the box or not. If she does not, then it is I who will stand at a grave disadvantage—

CROOM-JOHNSON. My Lord, I think an adjournment at this juncture would be the right—

O'CONNOR. (*angrily*) It would be most damnably wrong!—Forgive me, My Lord, but I am not exaggerating when I say that in this moment—this exact moment—lies the hinge of this entire trial. Any delay, even of half an hour, might be fatal to the cause of justice. In my view it is vital that my client goes into the witness box to give evidence on her own behalf, as she has the right and, I have told her, the duty to do. I believe and pray that if called upon now, she will go. With Your Lordship's permission. I therefore call Alma Rattenbury.

There is a pause. ALMA *enters, and walking as if in a daze, goes to the witness box. In the box a board is handed to her and a bible.*

CLERK. Take the book in your right hand and repeat the following words after me. I swear by Almighty God.

55

ALMA. I swear by almighty God.

CLERK. That the evidence I shall give to the court

ALMA. That the evidence I shall give to the court

CLERK. Shall be the truth, the whole truth, and nothing but the truth.

ALMA. Shall be the truth, the whole truth, and nothing but the truth.

O'CONNOR. You are Alma Victoria Rattenbury.

ALMA. I am.

O'CONNOR. Mrs. Rattenbury, how long were you married to your husband?

ALMA. Eight years.

O'CONNOR. By him did you have a child?

ALMA. Yes. Little John.

JUDGE. Mrs. Rattenbury, I can't hear you. Speak up, please. And please make sure the Jury can hear what you say.

ALMA. I'm sorry. I'm sorry.

O'CONNOR. Mrs. Rattenbury—little John, how old is he?

ALMA. Six—Six (*Louder*)

O'CONNOR. And you have been married twice before, I think?

ALMA. Yes.

O'CONNOR. By the second husband you had a child, did you not?

ALMA. Yes. Christopher.

O'CONNOR. You are fond of him, I think.

ALMA. Yes.

O'CONNOR. Very fond?

ALMA. . . . Very fond.

O'CONNOR. Now, Mrs. Rattenbury, I want you to tell me about your relationship with your husband. Since the birth of—

ALMA. Er—(*She looks towards the public gallery*)

O'CONNOR. Mrs. Rattenbury?

ALMA. No, I—

JUDGE. Is something wrong, Mr O'Connor?

O'CONNOR. I'm sorry, My Lord. An oversight on my part. If Your Lordship permits—

He turns to MONTAGU, *and murmurs . . . 'get the boy out of court, will you . . .'*

MONTAGU *nods and goes.*

I do apologise, My Lord. Now, Mrs. Rattenbury, would you say your married life was happy? . . . Mrs. Rattenbury!

ALMA. I'm sorry?

56

ALMA *looks at the court, then . . .*

O'CONNOR. Would you say your married life was happy?

ALMA. Well it was a bit—you know—

She makes a gesture indicating 'up and down'.

O'CONNOR. You had some quarrels?

ALMA. Not many. Only little ones, and always about money. He was a bit—well—stingy. I often had to tell him little fibs to get the bills paid.

O'CONNOR. Yes. Well, we'll come back to that.

MONTAGU *returns and nods to* O'CONNOR. ALMA *again looks into the court, but clearly* CHRISTOPHER *has gone.*

O'CONNOR. Mrs. Rattenbury, I want you to tell us now about your relationship with your late husband. Be quite frank, please. Since the birth of little John six years ago did you and Mr. Rattenbury live together as husband and wife?

ALMA. No.

JUDGE. Mrs. Rattenbury, I must ask you to speak much louder please. And please address your replies so the Jury may hear them.

ALMA. I'm sorry.

O'CONNOR. Since that time you did not live together as husband and wife at all?

ALMA. No.

JUDGE. Mrs. Rattenbury, you do understand what was meant by the question?

ALMA. Yes.

O'CONNOR. Did your husband have a separate room?

ALMA. Yes.

O'CONNOR. Was that at his suggestion or yours?

ALMA. Oh, his.

O'CONNOR. You would have been ready to continue marital relations with him?

ALMA. Oh yes, of course.

O'CONNOR. But he didn't want it?

ALMA. Well I think it was rather a question of the flesh being willing but the spirit being weak—

O'CONNOR. Er—the other way round I think?

ALMA. I expect so.

O'CONNOR. Now, between the months of November 1934 and March 1935 were you having regular sexual intercourse with Wood?

57

ALMA. Yes.

Again she has a quick look into the court.

O'CONNOR. And what attitude did your husband take to all this?

ALMA. None whatsoever.

JUDGE. You mean he didn't know of it?

ALMA. Oh, I think he must have known of it, My Lord.

JUDGE. Then he must have taken some attitude—even if it was one of tactful silence?

ALMA. I just don't think he gave it a thought.

The JUDGE *makes a heavy note.*

O'CONNOR. Now, Mrs. Rattenbury, I am going to take you through the events of the week that led up to your husband's murder and I want you to answer my questions with complete truth. You will, will you not?

ALMA *doesn't reply.*

JUDGE. Mrs. Rattenbury, you are under oath. You must reply fully and truthfully to Counsel's questions.

Again ALMA *doesn't reply.*

O'CONNOR. On Monday March 18—that is six days before the murder— did you ask your husband for some money? . . . Mrs. Rattenbury?

JUDGE. One moment please. Mrs. Rattenbury, you do understand, do you not, that having taken the oath to tell the truth, the whole truth, and nothing but the truth, you are in law in duty bound to do so. Do you understand that?

ALMA. Yes, My Lord.

JUDGE. Then be so good as to answer Counsel's question.

O'CONNOR. For how much money did you ask?

Pause.

ALMA. Two hundred and fifty pounds.

O'CONNOR. What little fib—to quote your words—did you have to tell him?

ALMA. That I was going up to London to have an operation.

O'CONNOR. And on the following day you went up to London?

ALMA. Yes.

O'CONNOR. And you stayed with Wood at an hotel in Kensington?

ALMA. Yes. The Royal Palace.

O'CONNOR. During that time did you give Wood some presents?

ALMA. Yes. A pair of silk pyjamas, a new suit, and then a ring for him to give to me.

58

O'CONNOR. Now it has been strongly suggested that there was some very sinister significance in this hotel visit only a few days before the murder. It has in fact been represented as a kind of premature honeymoon. What truth is there in that?

ALMA. Oh, none at all. It wasn't the first time we'd gone to a hotel, and he did love it so. He loved being waited on and called sir—

O'CONNOR. And you wanted to give him that pleasure?

ALMA. Yes.

O'CONNOR. And that was the reason for the presents?

ALMA. Yes.

O'CONNOR. And the ring to yourself?

ALMA. The ring was only a pretence.

O'CONNOR. A pretence of what?

ALMA. Well—like an engaged couple.

O'CONNOR. So this visit was no more than a whim, designed to give Wood pleasure. What about you? Did it give you pleasure too?

ALMA. No. It was terrible.

O'CONNOR. In what way terrible.

ALMA. Oh, rows.

O'CONNOR. Serious rows?

ALMA. Not on the surface. But underneath, of course, they were. You see he knew I was trying to finish it.

O'CONNOR. Finish the relationship?

ALMA. Yes.

O'CONNOR. Why?

ALMA. Well, it had got out of hand.

O'CONNOR. Had you told him that?

ALMA. I tried to often, but the difference in our ages made it so difficult. After we'd got back from London I was determined to say 'finish for good'—and mean it. I'm quite sure he knew that, which is why he was making my life hell . . .I'm sorry, My Lord. Dreadful . . .

JUDGE. Hell will do. Now I am not sure I have followed this. You say you tried to break the affair with Wood but were unable to—one of the reasons being the difference in your ages. Surely that very thing would make it easier?

ALMA. No, My Lord. Sorry, but it makes it harder.

JUDGE. But surely the older party must be the dominant party?

ALMA. Excuse me, My Lord, but to me it's the other way round.

Anyway it was with me and George. I think it must be with many people. Of course I don't know.

O'CONNOR. Now, Mrs. Rattenbury—

JUDGE. One moment please, Mr. O'Connor.

The JUDGE *finishes writing then signals* O'CONNOR *to continue.*

O'CONNOR. Mrs. Rattenbury. We come now to your return to the Villa Madeira two nights before the murder. Did your husband ask you any awkward question when you saw him?

ALMA. No. It was as if I'd never been gone.

JUDGE. He must surely have asked you about your operation?

ALMA. No, My Lord.

O'CONNOR. Anyway all was normal at the Villa?

ALMA. Oh yes. Very friendly.

O'CONNOR. How was Wood?

ALMA. Well he was a bit sulky. He'd wanted to stay on at the hotel, you see. But he perked up later.

O'CONNOR. You had intercourse that night?

ALMA. Oh yes, everything normal as you said.

O'CONNOR. Thank you. Now we come to Sunday, the day of the murder.

ALMA. Oh no. No. I can't—I . . .

O'CONNOR. One moment Mrs. Rattenbury, please.

ALMA. But I can't—I can't—

O'CONNOR. Please. Please.

ALMA *is silent.*

My Lord, in view of the obvious difficulties which I see your Lordship has noticed, I would crave your indulgence at this point to embark upon a somewhat unusual course. With Your Lordship's permission, I would like to quote certain passages from the signed statement entered by the prosecution yesterday, which was made by the prisoner Wood on the day of his arrest—Exhibit 27, My Lord.

JUDGE. But that is evidence against Wood. You are asking to use it on Mrs. Rattenbury's behalf?

O'CONNOR. Naturally, My Lord. I would hardly use it against her.

CROOM-JOHNSON. My Lord, I must most strenuously object to any part of the statement being read on behalf of Rattenbury. What cannot in law be used against her, must not in law be used for her. My learned friend should know that very well.

O'CONNOR. I really do not need lessons in law from prosecuting counsel. I do know that it is my duty to my client to use any evidence on her behalf that this court will allow—any evidence, of any kind, and from any source.

CROOM-JOHNSON. But My Lord, there are no precedents for such a—

JUDGE. Yes, yes, Mr. Croom-Johnson. It is plainly a matter for me. You are perfectly correct in saying that this proposed course is highly irregular—but having regard for the undoubted fact that the law always allows, and must allow, the greatest possible latitude to the defence in a capital charge, I will decide in favour of Mr. O'Connor.

O'CONNOR. (*plainly delighted*) Thank you, My Lord.

CROOM-JOHNSON sits, muttering . . . 'dangerous precedent . . .'

The lights fade to O'CONNOR *and more dimly on the* JUDGE.

O'CONNOR. I refer Your Lordship to paragraph three, in which Wood is describing the events of the murder. He says: 'They were up in her bedroom together—' That is, Mr. and Mrs. Rattenbury, My Lord.

JUDGE. I have it, thank you, Mr. O'Connor.

The light on the JUDGE *fades out.*

The light fades up on WOOD, *listening outside the bedroom door.*

O'CONNOR. When I went up with the tea the door was locked. So I listened outside, and then I heard them—kissing noises and 'darling'. And then I heard them doing it. I listened to them right through, then I heard them talking and getting off the bed, so I went into my room and waited for them to come out . . .

The lights come up on the Villa Madeira. WOOD *goes to his room. The bedroom door opens and* RATTENBURY *comes out, putting on his jacket.* ALMA *has a dressing-gown on. She helps him down the stairs, which he has to take very gingerly.*

ALMA. Gently does it, Ratz. That's right . . . So I'll tell the Jenks we'll be over tomorrow, shall I?

RATTENBURY. If they'll have us.

WOOD appears, a menacing figure at the top of the stairs. He is in his shirtsleeves.

ALMA. (*gaily*) Of course they'll have us. They're always asking us to stay. How long shall I say? A couple of days?'

RATTENBURY. It's a long way to go for a couple of days. Lot of petrol. Make it a week.

ALMA. All right, dear.

WOOD. (*calling*) Alma, I want to see you.

ALMA. (*looking up*) Come down then.

WOOD. (*commandingly*) Up here. Now.

RATTENBURY. (*muttering*) You shouldn't let him talk to you like that, Alma.

ALMA. (*shrugging*) He's in one of his moods—back in a jiffy.

She climbs the stairs. WOOD, *in a passion, grabs her wrists.*

WOOD. Why was that door locked?

ALMA. Locked? Was it?

WOOD. You lying bitch—

ALMA. (*laughing*) George, you *can't* think that me and Ratz—

WOOD *opens the door and looks inside.*

WOOD. Yes. Tidied up the bed now, haven't you? You were at it just now with him, weren't you? I heard.

ALMA. Oh George, you are a scream! Ratz, of all people. Oh, I'll die of laughing—

WOOD *hits her hard.*

(*Angry*) George, if you ever do that again—

WOOD. You'll what?

ALMA. Tell you to get out of this house and never come back—

WOOD *produces a revolver from his pocket.*

WOOD. I could kill you quite easily.

ALMA. (*calmly*) Yes I expect you could, dear, but not with Christopher's water pistol.

She takes it from him quickly.

George, are you all right?

WOOD. (*shouting*) Why was that door locked?

ALMA. Quiet, dear. Even Ratz could have heard that.

He hasn't. He is in the sitting-room placidly reading the paper.
The door was locked because it rattles when the window's open—as you should very well know. (*She strokes his face*) Silly boy!

She gives him back the pistol.

WOOD. Are you going to these people tomorrow?

ALMA. Yes.

WOOD. With me driving?

ALMA. Of course.

WOOD. I see. Where will I sleep?

ALMA. Oh, they've lots of room.

WOOD. In a servant's attic?

ALMA. Well, perhaps, but I'll try and see it's a nice one.

WOOD. And eat in the servants' hall?

ALMA. George, it's only for a week—

WOOD. And you and Ratz, with a nice big double bed—?

ALMA. (*angrily*) Stop this nonsense at once! At once, do you hear?

WOOD. Yes, Ma'am. Very good, Ma'am. Beg pardon I'm sure Ma'am.

She turns her back on him and picks up the phone.

ALMA. (*into phone*) Could you give me Bridport 31 please? This is Bournemouth 309.

WOOD. (*to her, and taking the phone out of her hand*) Listen, you cow. You're to go down there now (*Pointing to the sitting-room*) and tell him you're not going to the Jenks tomorrow—

ALMA. George, you're going to make me very angry.

WOOD. Because if you don't I'm going to do something very bad. Something very very bad.

ALMA. Put acid in that waterpistol and squirt it in my face? (*She takes the telephone. Into phone*) Hallo? (*To* WOOD) Go into the kitchen and help Irene with supper, there's a good boy.

Obediently he goes, half into shadow, and then turns to listen.
(*into receiver*) Hallo. Is that Mrs. Jenks? . . . Alma Ratten-bury . . . Ratz and I wondered if we could take you at your word and come over for a few days . . . (*To* WOOD) Go on, ducky—

WOOD. I'm warning you, Alma. Something really *bad*—

ALMA. (*into receiver*) Well I thought tomorrow, if you could have us—Oh, that *is* nice . . . Yes we'll drive over . . . I've a chauffeur now, you know. Lovely, see you soon. Goodbye.

WOOD *runs out.*

Fade out *except for the spot on* O'CONNOR, *and dimly on the* JUDGE.

O'CONNOR. Wood's statement continues :

The light *on the* JUDGE *fades out.*
I went to my Dad's and borrowed the mallet. Then I went back. I could see them through the French windows, playing cribbage. Then she went up to bed. So I went into the room and hit him three times on the back of the head with the mallet. Then I went into the garden and hid the mallet. Then I went up to bed.

The light *on* o'connor *fades and comes up on the Villa Madeira. In the sitting-room, very dimly seen, is the slumped figure of* RATTENBURY *in the armchair. Upstairs* ALMA *is in bed in pyjamas, reading.*

ALMA. (*calling*) George!

WOOD. (*off*) Yes.

ALMA. Where have you been all evening?

WOOD. (*off*) Out.

ALMA. What are you doing?

WOOD. (*off*) Getting undressed.

ALMA. You want to come in?

Pause.

> WOOD *appears in the passage dressed in silk pyjamas. He goes into* ALMA'S *room, and slips off his pyjamas, letting them drop on the floor.*

ALMA. (*lovingly*) That's no way to treat three guinea pyjamas, my lad—

He climbs into bed. She kisses him. He turns on his back.

WOOD. I'm in trouble, Alma. Real trouble.

ALMA. Real trouble? There's no such thing, that's what I always say—

He turns over again, his back to her, and begins to cry.

> This is a lovely world, and we're all meant to enjoy it. Now come on. Look at me—

WOOD. I can't.

ALMA. Well at least then tell me what it is.

WOOD. I can't . . . It's Ratz.

ALMA. What about him?

WOOD. I've—hurt him—

ALMA. You had a fight?

WOOD. Not a fight . . . I wish it had been a fight.

ALMA. Have you hurt him badly?

WOOD. Yes. Very badly.

Suddenly there is a hoarse sound from RATTENBURY *whose head falls forward.*

ALMA. (*rising*) Was that him?

WOOD. It must have been. I thought I'd killed him.

She sits up in bed.

ALMA. What have you done to him?

There is another sound from below.

ALMA. (*calling*) I'm coming, Ratz, I'm coming, darling.

She puts on a blue kimono, lying on the end of the bed. He clutches her arm.

WOOD. Don't go down.

ALMA. I must. If he's hurt badly I must help him—

WOOD. I've done for him, Alma. You won't get him back—

ALMA. (*running down the stairs*) I'm coming Ratz, darling. I'm coming.

She runs into the darkened sitting-room. After a moment she lets out a loud scream.

WOOD *gets back into his pyjamas and leans over the banisters again.*

IRENE *comes out of her room.*

IRENE (*to* WOOD) What's the matter?

WOOD. Don't know, I'm sure.

She gives him a suspicious glance, then runs down the stairs, just as ALMA *comes out of the sitting-room staggering from shock.*

IRENE. What is it?

ALMA. Ratz. Someone's hurt him Irene—Agh!! . . . Doctor O'Donnell. Run out and get Doctor O'Donnell. Quick—Irene—quick . . . Tell him Ratz may be dying.

IRENE *runs out of the front door. We still don't see* RATTENBURY *clearly, but as* ALMA *approaches the chair his body suddenly slumps out of it on the floor.* ALMA *gives a gasp and runs away. Then she kneels at his side.* WOOD *has come into the room.*

ALMA. Ratz—my darling Ratz—help's coming soon. Stay alive, please stay alive—Ratzie, can you hear me?

WOOD *has approached the body.*

WOOD. It's no good, Alma. I told you upstairs I'd done for him, and I have.

ALMA. Oh no, no—he isn't dead. He can't be. Ratz . . . Ratz . . .

WOOD *pours her a large whiskey, and makes her drink it. It makes her retch.*

Why did you do this? Why, why.

WOOD. I had to. He was stealing you away from me.

ALMA. Oh God, you little idiot. He wasn't stealing me—he couldn't have . . . Look, oh my God! He's—

She points to RATTENBURY'S *trousers, where he has fouled himself. Again* ALMA *retches.*

WOOD. I told you I was going to do something really bad—

65

ALMA. To *me*. I thought you meant to *me*.

She takes off her kimono, and covers RATTENBURY *with it.*

Oh God, poor Ratz. Why didn't you kill me?

There is a ring at the front door.

Go upstairs. Go to your room. Don't come down here unless you're sent for, and then know nothing about it. Nothing at all, do you understand?

There is another ring at the front door.

Go upstairs.

WOOD *turns to go.*

WOOD. What'll you tell them?

ALMA. I'll think something up. Coming?

O'CONNOR. 'I'll think something up' . . . 'I'll think something up'. And what she thought up was the ludicrous mad story she told the police. Was it the story of a sane, calm, balanced woman? Or was it not a story thought up in panic by a woman in a deep state of shock, aggravated by repeated doses of whiskey, and desperate at all costs to save the life of her lover?

CROOM-JOHNSON. You're addressing the Jury! My Lord, really I must object. Counsel is addressing the Jury.

JUDGE. Yes, I quite agree. Mr. O'Connor, that was highly improper. The time for your address to the Jury is not yet, as you very well know. That was really highly improper.

O'CONNOR. I'm so sorry, My Lord, you are of course quite right. I'm afraid I was momentarily carried away. I do apologise to my learned friend, and to you, My Lord.

JUDGE. Have you finished with Wood's statement?

O'CONNOR. Yes, My Lord.

JUDGE. And you propose to continue your examination on more conventional lines?

O'CONNOR. Indeed, My Lord.

JUDGE. Then first I must address a few remarks to the Jury, and try to make certain important matters clear. Ladies and Gentlemen of the Jury, I trust you understand that what you have just heard read to you is a statement made by the prisoner Wood, and cannot be used in any way at all as evidence against the prisoner Rattenbury. If you have heard anything you consider prejudicial to Mrs. Rattenbury, you must put it completely out of your minds. I trust that is clear. Very well, Mr. O'Connor, you may proceed.

O'CONNOR. Thank you, My Lord. Now Mrs. Rattenbury, I'm

66

going to ask you a very important question. Is there any part of that statement of Wood's that is in any way inaccurate or untrue?

JUDGE. Mrs. Rattenbury, you must answer the question.

O'CONNOR. Is there?

ALMA *shakes her head.*

O'CONNOR. Mrs. Rattenbury, is any part of that statement inaccurate or untrue in any way?

ALMA. . . . No.

O'CONNOR. None whatever?

ALMA. No.

O'CONNOR. Thank you. And what you thought up, was the ludicrous mad story that you told the police . . .

CROOM-JOHNSON. Is that a question?

O'CONNOR. It is a question. Mrs. Rattenbury, have you ever in your life suffered a greater shock to your mind, body and spirit than you suffered that night when you found your husband battered to death by your lover?

CASSWELL *and* CROOM-JOHNSON *are both on their feet.*

CASSWELL } (together) My Lord—
CROOM-JOHNSON }

O'CONNOR. —*Presumably* by your lover?

ALMA. No. Nothing ever—in all my life.

O'CONNOR. These stories of your dancing semi-nude making advances to policemen, playing the gramophone at full blast— did they or did they not come as a complete surprise to you when they were told to you as late as three weeks ago?

ALMA. Yes, they did.

O'CONNOR. And what was your over-riding emotion on hearing of them?

ALMA. Shame. Deep, deep shame.

Pause.

O'CONNOR. Mrs. Rattenbury, three last questions. Did you murder your husband?

ALMA. No.

O'CONNOR. Did you take any part whatever in planning his murder?

ALMA. No.

O'CONNOR. Did you, in fact, know a thing about it until Wood told you, in bed upstairs, that he had done it?

ALMA. No. If I'd known, I'd have prevented it.

67

O'CONNOR. Thank you. That is all.

He sits down. ALMA *starts to leave the box.*

CROOM-JOHNSON. (*getting up quickly*) Just a moment, Mrs. Rattenbury, you're not finished yet. I have some questions to ask you. In fact a great many questions.

The lights fade.

The lights come up *on* CROOM-JOHNSON'S *cross-examination of* MRS. RATTENBURY, *which has now been in progress for some hours. She is very tired.*

. . . Mrs. Rattenbury, just how old was Wood when you first invited him into the Villa Madeira as your lover?

ALMA. I didn't invite him—not in the way you mean. He insisted on living in—

CROOM-JOHNSON. *Insisted?*

ALMA. Why not?

CROOM-JOHNSON. But surely you could have resisted him easily, a boy of seventeen?

ALMA. Not easily at all. Ever since this case began the one thing I've heard is how I must have dominated this—boy. Well I can only say that if anyone dominated anyone else, it was George who dominated me—

CROOM-JOHNSON. Very interesting, but let us please stick to the facts. You have admitted, have you not, cheating your husband out of a considerable sum in order to take your lover up to London. Was that done under Wood's *domination*?

ALMA. It was his idea.

CROOM-JOHNSON. And the Royal Palace his choice of hotel?

ALMA. No. That was mine.

CROOME-JOHNSON. And whose idea was it buying the engagement ring?

ALMA. It wasn't an engagement ring.

CROOM-JOHNSON. Well, whatever it was, who suggested buying it?

Pause.

ALMA. I did.

CROOM-JOHNSON. Indeed. Now let us return once more to the evening of the murder. This purported conversation—this alleged confession of Wood's—took place in your bedroom?

ALMA. Yes.

CROOM-JOHNSON. But I understood that your sexual meetings usually occurred in Wood's room?

68

ALMA. Yes. That was because of little John sleeping in mine.

CROOM-JOHNSON. (*a shade wearily*) That night then little John was somewhere else?

ALMA. (*almost equally weary*) No. He was in my room.

There is a murmur in court. CROOM-JOHNSON *instantly perks alive. The* JUDGE *looks up. Even* O'CONNOR *looks unhappy.*

CROOM-JOHNSON. Little John was in your room?

ALMA. Yes, but sound asleep.

CROOM-JOHNSON. Your lover climbed into your bed with your little son in the same room?

ALMA. Yes, but he was sound asleep.

CROOM-JOHNSON. Used this to happen often?

ALMA. Well it had to sometimes, when Christopher was home.

CROOM-JOHNSON. Your lover would clamber into bed with you and you would indulge in sexual congress, with your six-year-old child in the same room?

ALMA. But he's a very sound sleeper.

CROOM-JOHNSON. A little child of no more than six summers—

O'CONNOR. My Lord, I fail to see how any of this is pertinent, unless of course my learned friend intends to call little John as a witness in rebuttal of his mother's testimony.

CROOM-JOHNSON. I find that remark in the most appalling taste—

O'CONNOR. And I find these constant references to little John's presence in that room—a cheeild (*he pronounces it so*) of no more than six summers—autumns, winters and springs come to that—I find these slurs on my client's moral character not only in appalling taste, but immoral, unfair, and entirely irrelevant. Who killed Francis Mawson Rattenbury? Isn't that what this court is convened to find out? It is surely not whether an act—or several acts—of sexual congress were committed in the distant presence of a heavily dormant child.

CROOM-JOHNSON. I trust my learned friend will have breath for his final address—

O'CONNOR. You need have no fear of that.

JUDGE. Gentlemen, please. This is becoming more of a cockpit than a court of law. I think Mr. O'Connor is right, Mr. Croom-Johnson. You have asked the witness a question—a perfectly relevant one in my view—and she has answered it. Pray let the matter rest there.

CROOM-JOHNSON. As Your Lordship pleases. Now I want to be absolutely fair to you, Mrs. Rattenbury—

O'CONNOR. (*muttering*) Fair?

CROOM-JOHNSON. When Wood, in bed with you, with your little boy in the corner—

O'CONNOR. My Lord.

CROOM-JOHNSON. I have not asked my question yet.

JUDGE. Please ask it, Mr. Croom-Johnson.

CROOM-JOHNSON. When Wood told you that night that he had hit your husband with a mallet, did you believe him?

ALMA. (*her voice a weary croak*) Not at first. No.

CROOM-JOHNSON. When you went downstairs and found your husband had indeed been hit on the head, did you believe him then?

ALMA. Well, one naturally would, wouldn't one?

CROOM-JOHNSON. You are here to answer my questions, not to ask them of me, Madam.

ALMA. I see. Well I did believe that he had done it then.

CROOM-JOHNSON. It is my duty to submit to you that you knew Wood had done it because you had encouraged him to do it? (*After a pause*) Well?

ALMA. I'm sorry. Was that a question?

CROOM-JOHNSON. It was a question, Mrs. Rattenbury, and a very important one.

ALMA. I thought I'd answered it. Still, if you want it again. (*Raising her voice*) I did not plot my husband's death. It was a great shock to me. I have never, in all my life, harmed a human being.

CROOM-JOHNSON. You have never harmed a human being?
Pause.

ALMA. (*on the edge of tears*) Not meaning to. Not till now.

The JUDGE *indicates to* CROOM-JOHNSON *to continue.*

CROOM-JOHNSON. Mrs. Rattenbury, in answer to my learned friend you said that if Wood had told you of his intention to murder your husband you would have prevented it. How would you have done that?

ALMA. I'd have told him not to dare do such a wicked thing.

CROOM-JOHNSON. Would that have been enough?

ALMA. The way I'd have said it it would.

CROOM-JOHNSON. But I thought you said he dominated you?
ALMA *does not reply.*
Well—supposing you had failed to persuade him, what would you have done?

ALMA. Gone to the police, I suppose.

CROOM-JOHNSON. But after the murder the police were all over the house. Why did you not tell them then?

ALMA. That was different.

CROOM-JOHNSON. Why?

ALMA. Well Ratz was dead and I suppose I felt responsible.

CROOM-JOHNSON. I beg your pardon?

ALMA. I said—I suppose I felt responsible.

CROOM-JOHNSON. Responsible. Thank you.

He sits down. O'CONNOR *gets to his feet, stifling a yawn—an old trick of his.*

O'CONNOR. (*languidly*) Only two questions, Mrs. Rattenbury (*Straight at* CROOM-JOHNSON)—Only *two*. By the word 'responsible' did you mean criminally responsible for your husband's murder?

ALMA. No.

O'CONNOR. Did you mean morally responsible for your lover's protection?

ALMA. Yes. That's exactly what I meant.

O'CONNOR. Thank you, Mrs. Rattenbury. That is all. That is the case for the defence of the Prisoner Rattenbury, My Lord.

JUDGE. Very well. I think that is a convenient moment to adjourn . . .

ALMA seems momentarily entirely ignored.

The LAWYERS *rise, stretch, and gather their papers, as the* JUDGE *perfunctorily nods three times, and leaves his chair.*

MONTAGU *has seen* ALMA *delaying in the box. He assumes rightly that she has not the physical strength to regain the dock—nor, perhaps, the moral strength either. He goes to the box through his preoccupied colleagues, and offers her his arm.*

MONTAGU. You did very well—very well indeed.

She seems not to have heard.

(*comfortingly*) Your job is done now.

ALMA. (*in a hoarse whisper*) Yes.

Fade out on the Court as ALMA *and the* LAWYERS *leave.*

The lights come on *in* MRS. DAVENPORT'S *sitting-room.* STELLA *is on the sofa, her head deep in a paper.* MRS. DAVENPORT *comes in.*

MRS. DAVENPORT. Has Tony called yet?

71

STELLA. Tony? No. He hasn't. Well? How was Mrs. Rattenbury?

MRS. DAVENPORT *stops, but doesn't reply.*

My God—she must have dominated that boy. Did she—

MRS. DAVENPORT *laughs harshly.*

What's so funny?

MRS. DAVENPORT. Yes, I suppose that's how it must seem.

STELLA. (*appalled*) Seem? Edie, you're not saying—

MRS. DAVENPORT. I'm not saying anything.

STELLA. Yes, you are. I know you too well. 'That's how it must
seem'. Edie—she's an awful, awful, woman. Sleeping with that
boy with her baby in the room—

MRS. DAVENPORT. What's that got to do with whether she
committed murder?

STELLA. Everything, I should have thought—

MRS. DAVENPORT. Then you don't know the law.

STELLA. It seems as if I don't know you.

MRS. DAVENPORT. Perhaps you don't. It's that word—dominated.
All the time, all the time that man was on at her: 'You were
twenty years older, Madam. Twenty years older. I put it to
you—you dominated that boy.' Do you know what she
answered? 'When an older person loves a younger, it's the
younger who dominates because the younger has so much
more to give.'

Pause.

STELLA. And you thought of Tony?

MRS. DAVENPORT. Of course.

STELLA. My God, to think that a murderess could go free just
because a jurywoman overloves a son who doesn't give a damn
for her.

Pause.

I'm sorry. I shouldn't have said that.

MRS. DAVENPORT. You did.

STELLA. Tony rang me, this afternoon. We had a talk. A long
one—

MRS. DAVENPORT. In which he told you he didn't love me?

STELLA. (*trying to embrace her*) Oh my God, darling. I only
said that because I was so damn angry with you.

MRS. DAVENPORT. Tell me what he said.

STELLA. Well, his father's got him a hundred per cent. It's a
love affair.

72

MRS. DAVENPORT. What does he want to do?

STELLA. Live with him of course.

MRS. DAVENPORT. For ever?

STELLA. Yes.

MRS. DAVENPORT. Supposing I fight?

STELLA. They'll fight back.

MRS. DAVENPORT. How?

STELLA. Tony will tell the Judge he prefers his father to you . . . Do you really want that? Of course he said he'd spend some of his holidays with you.

MRS. DAVENPORT. How kind . . .

STELLA. Darling, I do know how dreadful all this is for you. But you must try and forget about it, at least until this awful trial's over. Now, why don't you put your feet up, let me get you a drink. Darling, I know it's difficult for you, but you've a big responsibility tomorrow. You're not going to let this terrible business here cloud your judgement about that woman, are you?

MRS. DAVENPORT. No. I'm not.

FADE OUT.

Before the lights *come on again we hear the voice of* CASSWELL. *Then a spot illuminates his face, while another focuses on* ALMA'S.

CASSWELL. . . . when this boy met the woman he was an ordinary innocent English boy, four months later, what do we find? A confessed adulterer, a confessed thief, a confessed cocaine addict, utterly under the influence of an hysterical, lying, drunken woman of abnormal sexual appetites and apparently of no moral conscience whatever . . .

The voice merges smoothly into CROOM-JOHNSON'S.

CROOM-JOHNSON. . . . Can you believe a single word that such a woman says—self-confessed liar, self-confessed adulteress, self-confessed seducer of a tender youth of seventeen? . . . A woman who, by her own admission, robs her husband of a considerable sum, in order to indulge herself in a four-day sexual orgy at the Royal Palace Hotel, with a boy young enough to be her son . . .

The voice is merged with that of O'CONNOR.

O'CONNOR. Ladies and gentlemen. One of your number—I cannot, of course, mention her name, which would be most

73

improper, but I suppose I can say that she must be one of the foremost among you, a lady, evidently, of great moral courage and strength of character—she objected to serving on this case. 'Why?' asked His Lordship. 'Because' she replied, 'I am so prejudiced against Mrs. Rattenbury's moral character that I cannot be expected to give her a fair trial'. But how could she not be prejudiced against this woman? How could any one of you fail to feel disgust and nausea at the ensnaring and degradation of a helpless youth by a middle-aged woman of licentious and degenerate habits? But that is not the offence with which she is charged here in this court.

The voice merges into that of the JUDGE, *speaking in a matter-of-fact tone to the jury.*

JUDGE. Well, there it is. That is the woman. It is indeed difficult to find words in the English language in which you may see fit to describe her. But, members of the jury—the natural disgust you may feel for this woman must not—I repeat that—*must not* make you any more ready to convict her of the crime of murder. In fact it should, if anything, make you *less* ready to do so. Prejudice, dislike, disapproval, disgust, must have no part in your verdict. Well, that is all I have to say to you. You will now retire . . .

The lights *have* faded *to a* blackout. *A spot picks up the quiet white face of* ALMA, *which, during the whole of the foregoing judicial onslaught on her character has shown no sign of emotion whatever. Nor does it now as the* lights *come up in her cell.* JOAN *is with her.* ALMA *is sitting in a hard chair, immobile.*

JOAN. Look, dear, they may be a long time. Would you like to lie down? It'll have to be the floor—but I've had two blankets sent in, and a pillow—and I can make you quite comfy.

There is no reply from ALMA. *It is as if* JOAN *had never spoken.*

JOAN. Or I've brought some cards. How about a little game?

ALMA. (*at length*) Beg your pardon?

JOAN. (*showing the cards*) A little game, dear. We could have much longer to wait.

ALMA. No, thank you.

JOAN. Anything at all? Coffee? Tea?

ALMA. No.

JOAN. Not with a drop of something in it?

Pause.

Her stare continues unseeing.

Try not to fuss dear. What I always tell my ladies—

MONTAGU *comes in.*

MONTAGU. (*with a cheerfulness he doesn't feel*) Well, Mrs. Rattenbury—how are you feeling?

ALMA *seems unconscious of his presence . . .*

(*to wardress, in a low voice*) Is she all right?

JOAN. (*indignantly*) How could she be, after all that was said about her upstairs?

MONTAGU. I should have warned her.

He pulls a chair alongside ALMA'S *and touches her arm.*

ALMA. (*quite brightly*) Oh hullo, Mr. Montagu—

MONTAGU. You must try to understand why Mr. O'Connor had to say those things about you. They must have been horrible to hear—

ALMA. Not particularly.

MONTAGU. But you see, both Mr. O'Connor and the Judge, by saying all those foul things about you, *forced* the jury to concentrate their minds on only one thing—did you or did you not commit murder? Well, as we all know you didn't—

ALMA. Do you?

MONTAGU. Of course. So does Mr. O'Connor.

ALMA. And Christopher?

MONTAGU. And Christopher, most certainly.

ALMA. Then it really doesn't matter what the jury think, does it?

Pause.

MONTAGU. Mrs. Rattenbury, I have every hope that in a matter of hours—or even minutes—you will walk out of this place a free woman. If you do, what plans have you made?

ALMA *says nothing.*

JOAN. Her friend Irene Riggs is taking her to her home for a few days—

MONTAGU. Oh. That's good.

JOAN. She'll be all right there—she's fond of Irene.

MONTAGU. And then you must think of taking up your career again—

ALMA. My career?

MONTAGU. As a song-writer.

ALMA. Oh that—

JOAN. (*eagerly*) Yes, dear, you must. Just imagine how your songs will sell now.

ALMA *laughs harshly.* MONTAGU *gives* JOAN *a silencing look.*

WARDER. (*off*) Jury coming back.

ALMA. Mr. Montagu, I want to thank you—

MONTAGU. Don't. You have, and always will have, my admiration.

ALMA. Oh that's nice. That's the way men used to speak to me.

As they go out, fade into blackout. *In the darkness we hear the sound of the* LAWYERS *returning to Court. The* CLERK OF THE COURT *enters.*

The lights come up *on* MRS. DAVENPORT *and dimly on the* CLERK OF THE COURT.

CLERK OF THE COURT. Members of the jury, are you agreed upon your verdict?

MRS. DAVENPORT. We are.

The lights come up *on* ALMA *and* WOOD, *standing in the dock.*

CLERK OF THE COURT. Do you find the prisoner Percy George Wood guilty or not guilty of murder?

MRS. DAVENPORT. Guilty, but we should like to add a rider to that. A recommendation to mercy.

CLERK OF THE COURT. Do you find the prisoner Alma Victoria Rattenbury guilty or not guilty of murder?

MRS. DAVENPORT. Not guilty.

The court hears a storm of booing, hissing and shouts of 'shame!', but we do not hear it. Light fades up *on the* JUDGE.

CLERK OF THE COURT (*hardly heard*) And those verdicts are the verdicts of you all?

MRS. DAVENPORT. They are.

The storm of booing is apparently renewed. The light fades out *on* MRS. DAVENPORT.

JUDGE. This will not be tolerated.

The storm subsides.

CLERK OF THE COURT. Percy George Wood, you stand convicted of murder: have you anything to say why the Court should not pass judgement on you?

WOOD. (*with a smile at* ALMA) Nothing at all.

JUDGE. Percy George Wood, the jury have convicted you of murder, with a recommendation to mercy. That recommendation will be forwarded by me to the proper quarter, where it will doubtless receive consideration.

They hear cries from the gallery of 'Don't worry, boy! We won't let them do it!' etc.

Meanwhile my duty is to pass upon you the only sentence which the law knows for the crime of which you have been convicted.

The black triangle is placed upon the JUDGE'S *wig by the* CLERK OF THE COURT.

The sentence of the court upon you is that you be taken from this place to a lawful prison, and thence to a place of execution, and that you there be hanged by the neck until you are dead, and that your body be afterwards buried within the precincts of the prison in which you shall have been confined before your execution. And may the Lord have mercy on your soul.

The JUDGE *nods for* WOOD *to be taken down.* ALMA *fiercely grabs his arm as if she would stop him.*

WOOD. Goodbye, you silly cow.

WOOD *goes off.*

JUDGE. Let Alma Victoria Rattenbury be discharged.

The light fades out on the JUDGE.

The lights fade up on the court.

O'CONNOR *is warmly shaken by the hand by* MONTAGU, *less warmly by* CASSWELL, *not warmly at all by* CROOM-JOHNSON. ALMA *stands meanwhile, bewildered, in the dock.*

ALMA *is approached by* IRENE RIGGS, *her face wreathed in an ecstatic smile. She too embraces her.*

IRENE. I knew it! I never had a moment's doubt. Now here you are, darling. (*She unfolds a mackintosh*) Just slip into this. That's right. Now we'd better have the scarf.

ALMA *takes it off obediently, to have it replaced with a simple beret.*

Now just till we get home—

She slips on to ALMA'S *nose a large pair of horn-rimmed glasses.* There's a policeman waiting going to show us out of a special door.

O'CONNOR. (*turning*) Ah, Mrs. Rattenbury. I'm so very pleased—

IRENE. Come on, dear. That policeman's waiting.

ALMA *and* IRENE *leave the court.*

O'CONNOR. Well, Croom-Johnson, may I congratulate you on an admirable performance. Of course you had a hopeless case —but you fought it very well.

CROOM-JOHNSON. Thank you—I must warn you that I intend to raise the matter elsewhere of your directly appealing to a member of the jury by name—

O'CONNOR. By name?

CROOM-JOHNSON. Forewoman?

O'CONNOR. Fore*most*, dear fellow. Fore*most*. Your hearing's letting you down.

CROOM-JOHNSON. It was, in my view, unpardonable—and I will say so.

O'CONNOR. Really! You mustn't let a little set-back sour you, dear fellow. Been playing much golf lately?

CROOM-JOHNSON Not much. Excuse me. (*He goes*)

O'CONNOR. (*gleefully*) Bad loser. I've always said so.

CASSWELL. (*approaching*) Well, O'Connor. Magnificent. The boldness of it staggered me.

O'CONNOR. (*chuckling*) Yes. I took a risk or two.

CASSWELL. There was a moment when I actually thought you were pleading with the jury to have the woman burned as a witch.

IRENE *has appeared, breathless.*

IRENE. Mr. O'Connor—she's disappeared—Alma's disappeared—

O'CONNOR. (*his mind elsewhere*) Alma?

IRENE. She suddenly ran right across the street and disappeared—

MONTAGU. What happened?

IRENE. Just now. There was this bus, I thought she was going under it. I shouted to her—but she didn't seem to hear. She just ran and ran.

MONTAGU. She knows your address. She's probably going there.

IRENE. But she doesn't.

MONTAGU. Well, the best thing to do is to go back to where she left you. She's bound to come back when there's no one else around—

IRENE. No one recognised her I'm sure. Shouldn't I tell the police?

MONTAGU. There's not much they can do. I'll come with you.

They exit.

O'CONNOR. Really, women of that class do panic so easily.

The lights come up *on* MRS. DAVENPORT'S *flat.* STELLA *is standing belligerently facing the door through which* MRS. DAVENPORT *has just entered.*

78

STELLA. Well? What happened? Edie?

MRS. DAVENPORT *has gone straight to the drink tray, and poured herself out a large whiskey.*

MRS. DAVENPORT. Didn't you hear it on the news?

STELLA. Come on, Edith. I've only got a few minutes. I mean how did you let it happen? What was the voting?

MRS. DAVENPORT. Let's think . . . I was at the head of the table, which is where they put the forewoman.

STELLA. What's the matter with you? Are you drunk?

MRS. DAVENPORT. Yes, I am a bit. (*She takes a long swig*) Well, each person spoke up, and I took the votes down. That was my job, you see.

STELLA. The voting. How was the voting?

MRS. DAVENPORT. (*suddenly brisk*) Five for guilty, and six for not. *She replenishes her drink.*

STELLA. So your vote made it six all.

MRS. DAVENPORT. No. My vote made it seven-five. Then all the others gave way.

STELLA. Gave way to you?

MRS. DAVENPORT. Yes.

STELLA. In God's name, why?

MRS. DAVENPORT. Because she was innocent.

STELLA. Innocent?

MRS. DAVENPORT. Of murder.

STELLA. Innocent! Who was it who said that nothing was too bad for that woman, that she deserved lynching?

MRS. DAVENPORT. She may deserve that. She does *not* deserve hanging for a murder she didn't commit.

STELLA. What does that matter, for God's sake?

MRS. DAVENPORT. It matters to me.

STELLA. Well, what price your pretty little house in Bournemouth now.

MRS. DAVENPORT. But—but no-one in Bournemouth knows that I was on the—

STELLA. Oh, of course they did.

MRS. DAVENPORT. I see. Well, I'll have to stay on in this flat.

STELLA. Looks like it.

MRS. DAVENPORT. And I hate it.

STELLA. I know. I must go—(*At the door*) Poor St. Edith, what's to become of you?

She goes out. The lights on the flat partially fade, as MRS.

DAVENPORT *pours herself a large neat whiskey and then slowly sits.*

Meanwhile ALMA *stumbles to centre stage. She sits, and at length she gets a pencil and a few crumpled envelopes from her pocket.*

She starts to write.

The lights come up *on a little* MAN, *sitting at an insignificant desk. He reads quietly from a folder in front of him.*

CORONER. Coroner's report in the matter of Alma Rattenbury deceased. William Mayfield, labourer, of this parish of Christchurch, stated that at about eight thirty p.m. on June 4 he was walking across a meadow through which ran a stream. On the bank of the stream he saw a lady sitting and writing. He crossed the stream by a bridge and went down the bank the other side. As he did so, he looked towards her and saw the lady standing, a knife in her hand. He ran back towards her but before he could reach her she had stabbed herself in the body five or six times, three of the wounds penetrating the heart. When he reached her she was dead, her head lying in one foot of water . . . I do not propose to read all the documents found beside the body. Mostly they appear to be random thoughts scribbled in pencil on the backs of envelopes and suchlike—but here is one. It begins: 'I want to make it perfectly clear that no one is responsible for my action. I made up my mind during the trial that if George was sentenced to death I would not survive him—'

He looks up at an unseen court.

In this context I might mention as an unhappy chance that had Mrs. Rattenbury lived only a few more days she would have heard of the reprieve accorded to George Wood by the Home Secretary.

He turns to his folder.

Now here are what must be her very last words as the paper was found under her body with the pencil still on it.

ALMA. Eight o'clock. After so much running and walking I have got here. I should find myself just at this spot, where George and I once made love. It is beautiful here. What a lovely world we are in, if only we would let ourselves see it. It must be easier to be hanged than to have to do the job oneself. But that's just my bad luck. Pray God nothing stops me. God bless my children and look after them. One has to be bold to do this thing. But it is beautiful here, and I am alone. Thank God for peace at last.

MRS. DAVENPORT *gets up unsteadily carrying her whiskey. We now see she is really very drunk.*

MRS. DAVENPORT. (*suddenly shouting*) But I gave you life! . . . I gave you life! . . .

She sips her drink, shaking her head.

(*In her most Kensington voice*) And, might I say, at some considerable cost to my own? . . . Really, there's no justice . . .

She laughs and drinks.

ALMA *takes out* CHRISTOPHER'S *scout knife. As she looks at it, the* lights fade out.

LIBRARY
WEST KENT COLLEGE